Southern Living
Quick Fabric
Decorating
STEP-BY-STEP

Southern Living
Quick Fabric
Decorating
STEP-BY-STEP

From the Editors of
Decorating Step-By-Step

OXMOOR
HOUSE

Library of Congress Control Number: 2001-135820
ISBN: 0-8487-2556-5
Printed in the United States of America
Second Printing 2002

Decorating Step-By-Step Magazine
Editor: Julia Hamilton
Art Director: Amy Kathryn R. Merk
Homes Editor: Rob C. Martin
Lifestyle Editor: Majella Chube Hamilton
Associate Homes Editor: Sarah Jernigan
Assistant Homes Editors: Alicia K. Clavell,
    Alice Welsh Doyle, Nancy Staab
Editorial Assistant: Melanie S. Gaines
Copy Chief: Lady Vowell Smith
Copy Editors: Ann Garry, Paula Hughes,
    Linda Dunn Smith
Senior Photographers: Jean M. Allsopp, Van Chaplin,
    Tina Cornett, Art Meripol, John O'Hagan,
    Allen Rokach, Mark Sandlin, Charles Walton IV
Photographers: Jim Bathie, Gary Clark, William Dickey,
    Beth Dreiling, Laurey W. Glenn, Meg McKinney Simle
Production Coordinator: Leah Haney

Oxmoor House, Inc.
Editor-in-Chief: Nancy Fitzpatrick Wyatt
Executive Editor: Susan Carlisle Payne
Art Director: Cynthia R. Cooper

Southern Living® *Quick Fabric Decorating Step-By-Step*
Editor: Rebecca Brennan
Copy Editor: Cathy Scholl
Copy Assistant: Jane Lorberau Gentry
Editorial Assistant: Diane Rose
Editorial Intern: Megan Graves
Senior Designer: Emily Albright Parrish
Illustrator: Kelly Davis
Photo Researchers: Ginny Allen, Tracy Duncan,
    Laurl Self

Director, Production and Distribution: Phillip Lee
Production Coordinator: Leslie Johnson
Production Assistant: Faye Porter Bonner

Contents

Introduction

WELCOME

At **Southern Living** *Decorating Step-By-Step* magazine, we're delighted you've chosen for your bookshelf this beautiful book on creativity with fabric. Because of its focus on easy, affordable home design projects, you'll soon find this volume to be an indispensable source of ideas and inspiration.

We've included many simple designs that you can complete in a few hours. But, if you're feeling a little more ambitious, combine several projects, such as window treatment, slipcover, and pillow ideas, and fashion a delightful new look for an entire room. In no time your home will reflect your own talents, imagination, and sense of style.

We based this book (and its companion volume, **Southern Living** *Quick Decorating Step-By-Step,* published in 2001) on the format of our popular newsstand publication on creative home design. *Decorating Step-By-Step* magazine presents classic comfort, affordable ideas, and achievable style, all in the timeless *Southern Living* tradition.

With warm regards,

Julia Hamilton

Julia Hamilton
Editor, *Decorating Step-By-Step*
Homes Editor, *Southern Living*®

Start with a FABRIC YOU LOVE

Who among us hasn't felt the rush of immediate
attraction, the heart-stopping feeling of love at first sight?
We're talking about fabric, of course. Browse these pages
for ideas to create a look you'll adore.

SOFTEN *With* FABRIC

Don't be afraid to mix fabrics and create your own style.

Whether you are starting from scratch or freshening up an outdated look, selecting new fabrics can change the mood of any room. But when you look out into the sea of fabrics to choose from, you might begin to sink with fear. With such a beautiful, diverse array of fabrics, where do you begin? A little self-evaluation and planning will help you pull together an irresistible room, just as this homeowner did with the wicker furniture in her sunroom.

DECIDE ON STYLE
Begin by determining how formal or casual a look you want. In order to create a cozy sitting area, this homeowner chose a soft palette of colors to set the tone. From there she chose a lavender toile de Jouy fabric as the main focus of the room. To contrast with the formal toile de Jouy, she threw in a lavender gingham check and a moss-green stripe for a decidedly casual tone.

If you still find choosing fabrics scary, you may want to explore ready-made coordinates. Fabric displays often take the guesswork out of color coordination and pattern mixing by grouping fabric collections together. This path may prove a little less intimidating.

before

Arranged neatly in a sunroom, this sitting spot is now an attention grabber, thanks to a mix of lavender-and-cream toile and complementary stripes and checks.

BALANCE FABRICS

After you have found your fabrics, decide where to place them in the room for a balanced look. The most helpful advice is to keep it simple. Spreading patterns evenly around the room is usually the best strategy. Or you may opt for a more dramatic approach—using one pattern in a certain part of the room to draw the eye in that direction. This technique works well, as long as the fabric is balanced by a contrasting piece of furniture or accessory in another area of the room.

In this sunroom, the homeowner focused on the toile de Jouy. By using it on the settee, her largest wicker piece, the entire pattern repeat can be admired from most places in the room. Using the gingham check on the two chairs and ottoman that flank the settee lends a sense of visual harmony. Ready-made pillows in coordinating fabrics, including a complementary moss-green stripe, tie the room together while adding color.

Ready-made pillows in coordinating designs can make decorating a little less daunting. The soft lavender toile inspires the room's design elements.

Following the basic guidelines for mixing fabrics, the owner added matching cushions in a lavender gingham check to the armchairs and ottoman to create balance.

CONSIDER THE SHAPE

The structure of a cushion can make the style of a room. The homeowner followed the design of the wicker and filled the cushions with polyester Fiberfil to get a custom look. The pillows have rounded corners where the lines curve along the back of the furniture and mitered corners where the lines of the wicker are square. The back cushions were tufted to keep the filling in place and add a handsome detail.

A unique headboard made of an antique column and ceiling tiles is freshened with a matelassé coverlet and pillow shams.

PLAYING *With* TEXTURE

Artifacts combined with textured fabrics transform a plain bed and a dated brass table.

Architectural elements, contrasting textures, and complementary fabrics transform this bedroom into a retreat for Buffy and Zeb Hargett. A cool shade of hydrangea green sets the relaxing tone. Buffy, who treasures timeworn objects, displays her findings, then softens the crusty wood and metal with neutral-toned fabrics.

As an alternative to a new bed, Buffy found a column and tin ceiling tiles at a salvage yard, and she cleverly arranged the finds into a headboard. The weatherworn column was already split in half, so she secured the pieces to the wall at each side of the bed. Then she hung the tiles in a geometric design between the two columns.

The brass table was a perfect fit for the wall; however, the shiny brass and glass did not work with the room's look—a makeover was needed. A tobacco-colored linen sewn into a floor-length table skirt suits the comfortable mood. The dark linen contrasts with a creamy brocade runner that lays across the tabletop and drapes down the sides. (It also hides the seam in the skirt.)

before

Getting Started

TOOLS & MATERIALS

7 yards heavy linen

1 yard second fabric

scissors

sewing machine

straight pins

thread to match fabric

STEP-BY-STEP
(TABLE SKIRT & RUNNER)

This table skirt fits a 60- x 20- x 26-inch table.

1 CUT two panels from the linen to 116 x 38½ inches. Machine-stitch the lengths together with a ½-inch seam, and press. Hem all four sides with a 2-inch hem, and press. Position the cloth over the table, and crease the corners into pleats with your fingers. The corners should puddle on the floor. You can also iron in more permanent pleats, if desired.

2 CUT two pieces from the second fabric to 31½ x 18 inches to make the runner. Machine-stitch the two widths together with a ½-inch seam, and press. Machine-stitch a 1-inch hem on all sides, and press. Center the runner across the top of the skirt.

A cotton brocade runner layered over nubby linen covers a brass table to give a cozy feel to the bedroom.

Lighten up a dark table with
a layer of transparent vines.
This polyester sheer fabric
is hemmed on four sides for
a simple table cover.

SHEER
SOPHISTICATION

Invoke a breeze with refreshingly delicate fabrics.

The understated elegance of sheer fabrics conveys a tranquil mood. For a quick way to freshen up your interiors with soothing sheers, look for ready-made window panels and tablecloths, which are available in many home stores. If you want a custom pillow or table cover, shop upholstery fabric stores. You'll find a large selection of sheers to suit your budget.

(BELOW) Refresh a plain pillow by slipping it into a polka-dot case. Sew an open-ended cover, with a deep hem, slightly larger than the pillow.

(LEFT) Cover a bright pillow with sheer fabric for a softer look. Fashion a case with a front opening, and add ribbon ties for closures.

(RIGHT) Cool off any room by filtering sunlight through pale sheers, or enjoy the texture of the dotted swiss. These panels and others can be found in most home decorating stores. Some have tabs or casings for sliding on a rod; others can be hung with metal clip rings.

(OPPOSITE) A whimsical way to cheer up a window is with a panel full of pockets. Organdy flowers are randomly dropped in the pockets for a touch of color, but any lightweight object could easily be substituted; try seashells, clippings of real blooms, or color photo negatives.

TRENDY TICKING

Wake up to the beauty of this old-fashioned fabric.

No longer is this heavy cotton fabric hidden beneath the sheets. People are proudly displaying these simple striped patterns on chairs and sofas, pillows, bed covers, and curtains. Antique dealers offer vintage fabrics, and reproduction fabrics are available at upholstery shops.

It's no wonder this fabric is becoming popular—it's durable, it's affordable, and the classic stripes come in a variety of colors that will coordinate with just about anything. Designers are teaming these fabrics with plaids, florals, and toiles. Pick up some swatches from your local fabric store to see what colors work in your home, then try some of these ideas.

(BELOW) Rich reds and natural shades are coordinated for custom shams with buttons and ties. To create your own, measure a pillowcase, and cut ticking to size allowing for seams. Add a 5-inch border of complementary fabric, make buttonholes, and attach buttons or finish the edge with cording and 1½-inch-wide ties. Dress up a plain table skirt by hemming a square of ticking for a second layer. Slipcover a lampshade with a hemmed piece of fabric that is simply tied on with braided raffia or ribbon.

(ABOVE) A no-frill pew cushion and a simple pillow are stuffed with shredded foam to give a soft, downlike look. Seam wrong sides together, leaving a small opening; then turn right side out. Drop shredded foam into the opening for desired plumpness. Hand-sew the opening closed.

(ABOVE) Cut a long rectangle, and hem all sides for a slipcover. Attach brass grommets, and use twill tape to secure the slipcover to the chair.

(LEFT) Twenty-inch squares in a variety of stripes are hemmed to create colorful napkins for casual entertaining. Ticking is great for the tabletop because it's durable and washable—sew matching place mats, or stitch a tablecloth.

A tailored skirt in blue-and-natural ticking dresses up a small table. To customize a similar skirt for your table, draw a paper pattern of the top of your table and the skirt. Add an extra 8 inches for every pleat. (We have a pleat on each corner and one in the middle of the two longer sides.) Cut the fabric, allowing for seams and hem. Insert cording when stitching top to skirt. You can purchase complementary cording or cover cording in ticking.

TIMELESS TOILE

This lively fabric is at home in a variety of settings.

Toile refers to the printed fabric, normally one color over a lighter background, that was introduced in France in 1760. The patterns depicted historical scenes or pastoral landscapes and were instantly successful. When machine printing with engraved copper rollers was developed, mills produced toiles with crisper details and in greater quantities. Wallpapers were added to coordinate with toile designs—traditionally red, blue, black, green, or plum—on a cream background.

The English adapted the printing technique, and soon the toile rage reached this country, where homes sported motifs featuring nature and mythology. Toile fabrics and wallpapers never completely disappeared from traditional decorating, although patterns have waxed and waned in popularity. With the current emphasis on lighter interpretations of conventional toile designs, it is a popular choice for virtually any room.

Interior designer Barbara Johnson Irvine chose a black-and-white toile for the walls, furniture, and window treatments in this luxurious master bedroom suite in Atlanta. Bedroom walls are upholstered with the fabric, and at each window, swagged valance caps draw draperies. The duvet cover is made of the same fabric, and coordinating sheets are in a black-and-white check pattern.

The black-and-white theme continues in the adjoining bath. Arched openings frame the whirlpool tub, and the windows are dressed in a traditional, fringe-trimmed treatment.

Black-and-white toile window treatments add elegance to the bathroom.

Country French style translates into a luxurious master retreat with upholstered toile walls and a fruitwood sleigh bed.

This handsome guest suite gains much of its energy from the creative interplay of ticking and toile fabrics and wallpapers. The ticking pattern predominates in the bedroom, while the toile design prevails in the adjoining bathroom. (To make a toile duvet cover, see pages 130-133.)

IDEAS THAT WORK

•Use toile to create accents for a room, instead of making it the predominant fabric. Pillows covered in toile, for example, mix well with lacy bed linens.

•Combine toile with an inexpensive fabric, such as ticking or some other stripe, that matches the colors of the toile.

•Frame leftover fragments of the scenic fabric, and hang them in a hallway or other adjoining area.

(ABOVE) In the bathroom, the toile pattern is repeated in the wallpaper and on the balloon shade.

(LEFT) Open space below the countertop saves the effort—and expense—of installing cabinets. The skirt of toile fabric is interlined for fullness. Baskets and storage units on casters hide behind the skirt. Tole planters and framed prints add black accents.

(**ABOVE**) In the dining room, crisp checked fabric sewn into chair covers and draperies creates a cheery counterpoint to the toile-covered walls, repeating the black-and-white theme. The vibrant rug anchors the room.

(**RIGHT**) Chair slipcovers in the living room are made of black-and-white ticking. Chair pillows and an upholstered ottoman in black-and-white toile balance the striped fabric and add visual interest.

CURTAIN CALL

Window treatments are the icing on the cake, the cherry
on the sundae. Here's where a perfect pairing of fabric and
design will allow your room's personality to really shine.
Following are some ideas for award-winning charm.

Fresh
WINDOWS

Weary of facing a blank window every day? Stitch these informal curtains from an attractive fabric.

The beauty of this window treatment lies in its simplicity: Ties at the top of lined panels hang from knobs mounted on the window frame. Placing the curtains over lace sheers or wooden blinds will add privacy, while enabling you to leave the curtains open.

You can use any kind of knob that has a screw attached. Mount one knob at the center of the window frame; place others at the left and right edges. Then fill in with knobs placed at 6- to 10-inch intervals on the frame.

Use one width of fabric per curtain panel on small windows (30 to 36 inches wide). Add a half or full width for each panel on wider windows. Generally, each panel should be at least 1½ times the width of the space it covers.

To determine the length of the curtain panels, measure from the floor to the knobs. If you want the fabric to gather gracefully on the floor, add a foot or more.

You can determine the amount of fabric needed per window by counting the number of widths desired and multiplying this number by the panel length. You'll also need an identical amount of lining fabric; it should be the same width as your drapery fabric.

Be sure to purchase extra yardage for matching the repeats (designs) in the drapery fabric. Also purchase ⅔ yard of either lining or drapery fabric for each four pairs of ties. For each panel, you'll need a pair of ties to loop over each knob.

Getting Started

TOOLS & MATERIALS

yardstick or tape measure

knobs

drapery fabric

lining fabric

scissors

straight pins

thread

sewing machine

iron

ironing board

Each curtain panel is made from 1½ widths of 54-inch-wide fabric. Looping two pairs of ties on one knob near the center of the panel creates extra fullness.

Extra drapery fabric was used to make this accent pillow for the chair.

1 CUT drapery fabric and lining fabric to the previously determined curtain panel length. (When using more than one width of patterned fabric per panel, remember to match repeats. Patterns will also need to match where panels meet at center of window.) If you are using more than one width per panel, place long edges of widths of drapery fabric right sides together, and machine-stitch. Then place widths of lining fabric right sides together, and machine-stitch.

2 PLACE lining fabric and drapery fabric right sides together. Pin together along left, right, and bottom edges. Machine-stitch ⅝ inch from edges. Remove pins, turn drapery panel right side out, and press. At top edge, press ⅝ inch of drapery fabric and lining fabric to inside.

3 MEASURE and cut two 6- x 24-inch pieces of either drapery fabric or lining fabric for each pair of ties. Fold each strip of fabric in half lengthwise. Stitch down long edge and across one end, ⅝ inch from edge of fabric. Turn strips right side out, and press. Pin pairs of ties together, matching raw edges at ends. At left and right sides of drapery panel, insert 1 inch at raw ends of a pair of ties between drapery fabric and lining fabric, and pin in place. At top edge, pin additional pairs of ties at equal intervals. Stitch ¼ inch from top edge of drapery panel. Remove pins.

4 HANG drapery panel by looping a pair of ties over each knob and tying them into a bow.

(RIGHT) Curtain ties are made from the lining fabric. Two pairs of ties were left unattached, creating decorative folds in the curtains.

TRANSFER MAGIC

Vintage postcards of faraway places are your passport to stylish windows. Read on to see how easy the trip can be.

Use the copier to apply a mirror image of your postcard to the transfer paper, s that when you transfer it to the fabric, i faces right side up.

Window sheers gain instant glamour when pictures of distant locations dance across them. Adding images to gauzy fabric is simple with this quick-transfer process.

Purchase white or light-colored drapery sheers from a department store, bed-and-bath shop, or home-furnishings catalog. The sheers shown here have fabric tabs that are slipped onto a copper rod purchased from a plumbing supplier. You can also hang sheers from hooks or conventional curtain rods.

First, collect interesting old postcards of various destinations. You can usually find them in secondhand shops and at antiques malls. You can also use any other kinds of images for this project, but small ones are easiest to transfer.

At a copy center, have the postcards photocopied onto transfer paper. (This type of paper is fed into a copier by hand, and it enables you to transfer copied images to fabric.) Cut each image from the transfer paper and, one at a time, place them facedown on the sheer fabric. Press with a warm iron, and remove the paper backing. Hang sheers from hooks or a rod.

To accent your drapery sheers, display a scrapbook of old postcards nearby. Attach the postcards using photo corners for a vintage effect.

STEP-BY-STEP

1 PURCHASE several sheets of transfer paper at a crafts store or a copy center. (Be sure to follow instructions for your brand of transfer paper.) You can use either a black-and-white copier or a color copier. Because the final transfer will be a mirror image of the original, activate the copier's mirror-image function to reverse your copies. Copy several postcards at a time onto a sheet of paper.

2 CUT the copied photos apart and trim away unwanted areas. Preheat an iron to the temperature recommended for your transfer paper. Place the transfer facedown on the fabric. Place an old piece of clean, white fabric over the transfer so it doesn't burn. Press iron firmly for 15 to 20 seconds onto transfer, repeating until entire transfer has been ironed. Carefully peel backing away from fabric. Repeat procedure with remaining transfers.

A *Light* TOUCH

Sheer fabric can dress up an empty window and still give a room plenty of sunshine.

In this sunny room, it would be a shame to cover any of the windows with heavy drapes. In order to let the sun shine in and to be consistent with the already-established garden theme, we chose this sheer botanical print.

We simply used a single length of sheer fabric and secured it on small nails in the top of the window frame. Easy bows made of raffia covered our work and added another natural element.

You can choose from a wide variety of sheer fabrics to coordinate with your home's decor. Embellish the top of the window with raffia as we did, or try colored ribbons and tassels.

(ABOVE) Coordinating fabrics used to cover the chair cushions enhance the botanical theme created by the window treatment.

(LEFT) Raffia bows hide the nails used to secure the fabric to the window. You can find raffia at crafts stores and in the gift wrap section of large discount stores.

QUICK CURTAINS

Loosely hang sheer white fabric panels from metal clips for a soft and easy window treatment.

Try this quick idea to give any room in your home an updated look. With inexpensive cafe rods, a little spray paint, and a few yards of scrim (loose-weave cotton fabric), you can fashion this window treatment for less than $30.

Cafe rods and curtain clips—which usually come in a brass finish—are available at fabric shops and home-center stores. With flat black enamel spray paint, you can quickly give them the look of iron.

Purchase enough yardage to allow each drapery panel to puddle at the floor. There is no finishing work to do to the sides; the selvage (the finished edge on either side of the fabric) forms a natural hem. A stitched hem is required only at the top and bottom of each length.

Attach fabric panels to the rod with clips, and your new look is complete.

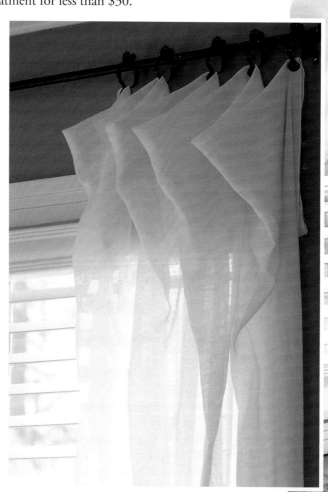

ROOM AT THE TOP

*If your window is a nice architectural feature
or you especially enjoy the view, why cover it up?
Just get fancy with fabric instead.*

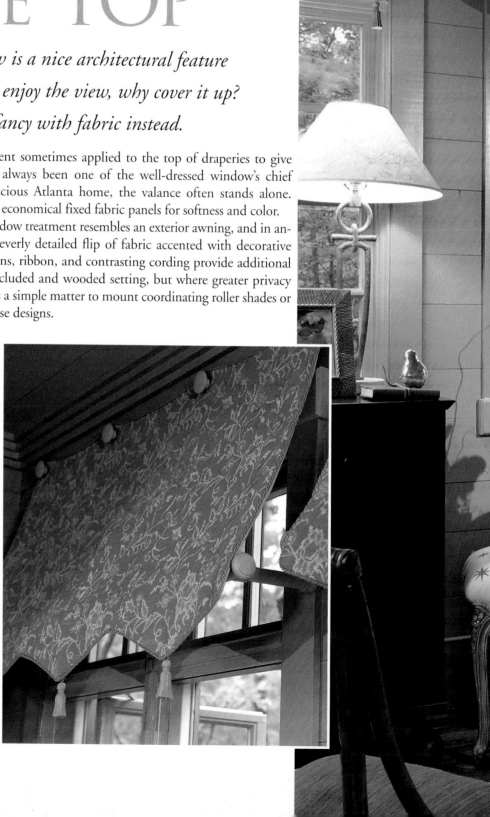

The valance, a fabric treatment sometimes applied to the top of draperies to give a more finished look, has always been one of the well-dressed window's chief accessories. But at this spacious Atlanta home, the valance often stands alone. Or it may be teamed with economical fixed fabric panels for softness and color.

In one informal area, the window treatment resembles an exterior awning, and in another it takes the form of a cleverly detailed flip of fabric accented with decorative hooks and tassels. Raffia, buttons, ribbon, and contrasting cording provide additional interest. The house enjoys a secluded and wooded setting, but where greater privacy and light control are desired, it's a simple matter to mount coordinating roller shades or mini-blinds behind most of these designs.

OUTSIDE IN

With its casement windows opened to admit lots of fresh air, the sleeping porch captures the feeling of a rustic cabin. The window treatments are cleverly styled to resemble exterior awnings. At each window, a lined fabric panel is edged in cording and hung from wall-mounted wooden knobs painted to match the walls. Tassels accentuate the points at the lower edge of the fabric. A U-shaped configuration of painted PVC pipe mounted on the window frame holds the awning at a fixed distance from the wall.

Painted drawer pulls support the fabric, while a PVC pipe framework gives the awning its shape.

STRAW POLE

The kitchen's window treatment hangs above eye level to preserve views of the wooded landscape. A spiraling iron rod mounted between the cabinets provides support that looks substantial, yet not heavy. Matching iron rings connect to a valance that's made of natural linen and edged in checked fabric. At the top, the fabric that's gathered at each ring is accented with a cutting of raffia. The bias edging at the bottom adds variety.

(RIGHT) Several dozen strands of raffia were wrapped around each curtain ring, then tied with additional pieces.

GET THE POINT

(ABOVE) This stylish swath of fabric was designed so that its points occur at even intervals on the window. (Note that the center point falls slightly below the others.) For this mudroom, designer Sherrill Holt used the colors of bark, nuts, and moss for a muted palette. Because the room doubles as a flower room and potting area, the choice of fabric depicting seed packets and other garden images is especially fitting. At each side, the dark green lining is turned back for visibility. The valance falls gracefully from leaf-shaped hooks mounted below the crown molding. Natural-colored tassels provide a jaunty finishing touch.

The artfully draped and pleated horizontal valance tops fixed drapery panels. Fabric-covered buttons accentuate the points on the valance. Both are sewn from plaid silk.

A Versatile WINDOW TREATMENT

Layered swags make it easy to create fresh style in seconds.

When her clients weren't ready to commit to a color scheme for their remodeled kitchen and breakfast room, Bitsy Duggins had the answer. "The room was neutral, and they really wanted to keep it that way for now," explains the Metairie, Louisiana, interior designer. "But they have an older New Orleans house, and the ceilings and windows are tall. We felt we needed to have some fabric."

As a solution, Bitsy designed a classic window treatment of fixed side panels, cascades, and a loosely draped top swag. For an instant change, she layered a second, colorful swag from a length of unlined fabric—and added rope trim.

To create the basic tailored look, Bitsy chose a 54-inch-wide, off-white cotton denim fabric. The material has enough body to hang properly without being lined. For the double

window shown here, 4 yards of fabric were used for the top swag, 4 yards each for the pair of decorative cascades, and 7½ yards for the fixed side panels. (Measurements, of course, vary depending on the height and width of a window.)

The cascade and the side panels are attached with self-fastening strips for simple installation and removal. The swag is casually draped over wooden knobs. A second length of unlined fabric, here a silk plaid, is placed over the swag, adding color and pattern. The ends of a length of rope, purchased from a neighborhood hardware store, are unbraided and knotted to add a tassel-like decorative trim.

"The best thing about this treatment is that it's so easy to change with the season or whenever you want a different look," Bitsy says. "Having an option like that is a lot of fun, too."

Constructed in sections from unlined denim, this window treatment proves a sophisticated look can be economical too.

An extra length of fabric instantly dresses up this tailored swag and cascade window treatment. Rope trim adds the finishing touch.

REEL SIMPLE

A small space calls for big creativity and some out-of-the-ordinary materials.

A window located in a difficult space left Nashville homeowners Laurel and Louie Buntin casting about for a drapery design for their son's room. "The space is so tight and the window so high that there wasn't a lot of room for a big window treatment," recalls Laurel. The Buntins achieved the privacy they sought with blinds and enlisted the help of local designer Ginger Kelly to tackle the valance.

"Louie graciously donated two of his childhood fly rods. We snipped off the ends, attached them to the board, and used them as drapery rods," Ginger says.

The design is simple but effective. Cafe rod brackets, mounted to the wall, were used to secure the fly rods. For added stability, the rods were wired together.

The valance is made of overlapping triangles sewn from inexpensive fabrics—a fishing-fly motif for the center of the triangles and plaid for the trim. The pieces are attached directly to the fishing rods with tab ties. For a no-sew option, Ginger suggests creating the same look by using heat-activated tape (found at local fabric stores).

The fabrics spawned a theme for the decor, and now, as 9-year-old Caldwell will attest, his room is a fisherman's paradise.

Heirloom fishing rods serve as a drapery rod for this fanciful bedroom valance.

Crowned in DIAMONDS

A canvas valance tops traditional draperies
with surprising sophistication.

If you know your math, you can make a striking valance for your window. It takes only 1 yard of canvas (found at art-supply stores) and a small amount of acrylic paint. We mixed four shades of green and beige to match the fabric panels. These steps are for a 50- x 26½-inch valance. Make necessary adjustments to fit your window.

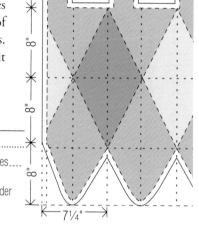

Cut lines _____
Guide lines ....
Hem & paint lines ....

To hem, turn under ¾ inch.

Getting Started

TOOLS & MATERIALS

1 yard of primed canvas (53 inches wide)

painter's tape or masking tape

acrylic paint in four colors

clear satin varnish

brushes in several sizes (¼ to 1 inch)

hot-glue gun and glue sticks

STEP-BY-STEP

1 LAY 1 yard of 53-inch-wide primed canvas flat on a work surface, primed side up. Following the illustration above, transfer the pattern using a ruler and pencil to the primed side of the canvas. The length of the tabs may need to be adjusted depending on the diameter of your rod.

2 TAPE off the diamond shapes for the first color. Apply three coats of paint; allow to dry, and carefully remove the tape. Repeat the process for the remaining three colors. Once the entire canvas is painted and dry, apply a protective coat of clear satin varnish.

3 CUT out the valance, following the cut lines in the illustration. Turn edges under where hem lines are designated, and use hot glue to secure hem. (When folding hem of bottom points to underside, you may need to trim the edge so that they just meet and don't overlap.) Fold hanging tabs to the back of the valance, and glue ends into place.

TEA-STAINED SHADE

A do-it-yourself window treatment is easy when
the decorative effect is created by the fabric.

Window treatments that solve problems are always a plus. You expect them to decorate a room, but when they also hide an unsightly view or filter harsh light, you get your money's worth.

Modern lightweight sheers are one choice that will accomplish all three tasks—a pretty look, privacy, and pleasant light. Today, many sheers are manufactured with a variety of embroidered designs integrated in the fabric, adding interest to an otherwise plain organza, cotton, or chiffon background. And best of all, they are not transparent, so light filters in while the room remains private.

For the powder room shown here, only one piece of fabric was used. Because the view was uninspiring, the treatment covers the entire window. Looped cording attached to the top hangs from upholstery tacks to keep it in place. Using sheers on windows is an old-fashioned idea, and this updated version exudes an air of aged sophistication. The fabric was originally a crisp white, but it was stained with tea to give it the lovely quality found in older, more delicate fabrics. Here's what we did to create this look.

STEP-BY-STEP

1 MEASURE the inside window dimensions; cut fabric to size. This window is 23 x 32 inches, so 1 yard of 54-inch-wide fabric was used.

2 FINISH each edge with a narrow shirttail hem. If you don't have a sewing machine, an iron and fusible web binding will also work.

3 ATTACH cording to the top with a machine zigzag stitch or baste by hand, adding loops every few inches.

4 STAIN white fabric with tea for an aged effect, if desired. (See box at right for instructions).

5 MEASURE and mark where tacks should be placed on the window frame, using loops as a guide. Nail tacks into frame. Hang treatment by placing loops around tacks.

Getting Started

TOOLS & MATERIALS

embroidered sheer fabric

tea bags (optional)

window shade cording (in fabric stores with window treatment hardware)

upholstery tacks

TEA-STAINING FABRIC

The fabric was a crisp white when purchased, but it was stained with tea for an antique look. The process is simple and should be harmless to most fabrics if soaked for the right amount of time. Prewash fabrics, and test samples first to ensure the right degree of stain.

1 FILL a standard-size washing machine halfway with hot water.

2 ADD six large tea bags. We used standard iced tea bags, but any type will do. Allow the tea to steep and cool. Note: Different tea varieties will produce different stain colors.

3 PLACE prewashed fabric in machine with tea, and let soak. The color will darken according to amount of time soaked, so check every few minutes. (The fabric shown here soaked for two hours.)

4 REMOVE fabric, and rinse. Hang to dry. Let washing machine drain; then run a standard cycle without clothes to remove any traces of tea.

This silk sheer window covering is a version of an outside-mounted Austrian shade. It provides privacy while the unlined fabric allows sunlight to filter inside.

MADE *in the* SHADE

A little goes a long way when it comes to these easy window treatments.

Shades make versatile window coverings. They can ensure privacy, control light and energy, or simply add a decorative element. Hardworking and good-looking, they can be designed in a multitude of fabrics and styles and are generally easy to maneuver and position.

Most shade designs use a minimal amount of fabric, making them economical problem solvers because they add interest and beauty with little investment. Because their finished width is usually equal to that of the window frame, they are an option for windows with little or no wall on either side.

Chintz fabric works wonders for a tailored window. Crisp, lined, and fixed in position, the treatment softens windows in a bath filled with textured materials. This shade's function is to add beauty and sophistication.

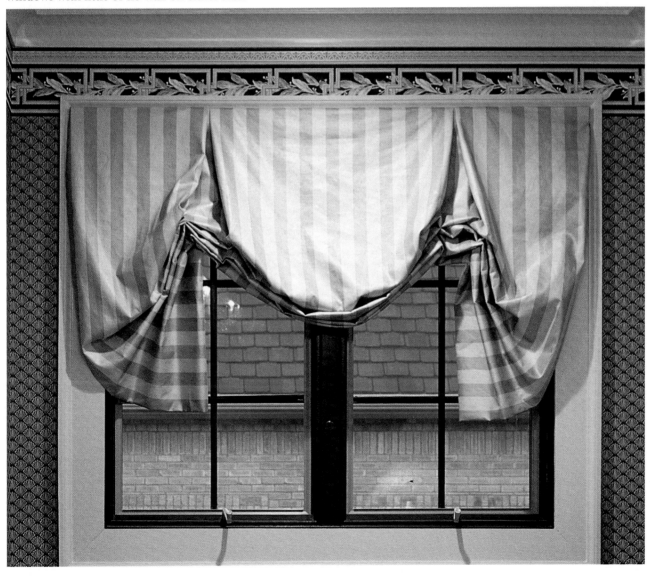

EASY *Embellishments*

These creative ideas offer easy ways to add

pizazz to plain shower curtains.

A bath is a personal haven, a place for retreating and pampering. An essential part of this room is the shower curtain, which provides privacy and water protection around the shower and tub areas. But shower curtains can present a design problem for the novice.

Relax! Even a beginner can use these tips for embellishing shower curtains and giving the bath an attractive, finished look. Each solution begins with a standard solid-colored curtain (60 x 72 inches), enhanced with stylish details that do not require a professional sewing room.

EASY ELEGANCE

Take advantage of leftover fabric used on window treatments. With the addition of a 12-inch kick-pleated ruffle and fringe on the bottom, plus 8-inch tabs on top, this curtain now takes on new height and becomes the focal point of the room. The first curtain rod installed is level with the window valance, while the second one holds the vinyl liner at normal height.

(ABOVE) Lengthening the curtain makes a dramatic change to this bath. Tabs placed over existing holes are attached with buttons covered in the same fabric. A simple pleated ruffle topped with decorative trim anchors the curtain.

CHIC SEW-ONS

Fringe and beads draw attention to this once plain curtain. Three decorative trims were sewn across the curtain, beginning approximately 18 inches from the top. Two trims were sewn ½ inch apart; the second trim also attaches the beaded fringe to the curtain. Trims, ribbons, buttons, and other accents are abundant at fabric shops, crafts centers, and even discount stores. Be creative—the possibilities are endless, and so is the fun.

LOVELY LAVENDER

This classic look is achieved with less than a yard of fabric. A small plaid pattern on the curtain rings and buttons adds interest to the tone-on-tone shower curtain. Covered buttons are attached just below the existing holes. The curtain ring covers were made from 14-inch fabric strips that were shirred over the rings before they were attached to the rod.

SPLISH, SPLASH

Here is a fun and playful way to bring some excitement to your child's bath time. Brightly colored washcloths, ribbon, buttons, and fringe sewn on this curtain not only add color but provide a home for tub toys and other items as well. The fabric strips and buttons sewn around the washcloths add support to the new pockets.

Brighten up bath time by adding some fun touches to your child's shower curtain. Fabric strips support the washcloth pockets.

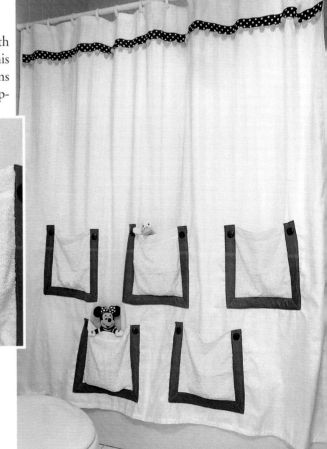

SKIRTING
the Issue

Dressing a table sets a mood like nothing else can. A dreamy sheer fabric says romance, a bold stamped design is whimsical, while a heavy, fringed cloth imparts classic character. Change the look as often as you change your mind with our easy ideas for tables.

SHEER
Romance

Use swirling layers of iridescent fabric to set a beautiful stage for your next gathering.

Whether it's a wine-and-cheese affair or an array of sinful desserts, these beautiful tablecloths will be the talk of the party. Richly hued sheer fabrics, swirled and layered on a tabletop, provide the perfect backdrop for an elegant buffet. Instructions for our sheer tablecloths or a simple no-sew version are on the following pages. Either way, you're set for a stunning table.

Wine and cheese take center stage against the backdrop of our blue-and-gold tablecloth with mitered bands, shown here layered atop the light-blue hemmed tablecloth.

STEP-BY-STEP
(BLUE-AND-GOLD TABLECLOTH WITH MITERED BANDS)

1 MEASURE the length, width, and drop of your table (ours is 3 feet wide and 8 feet long, with a 30-inch drop). Decide how much of a fabric puddle you prefer (ours is 6 inches). Determine the width of the mitered band (ours is 27 inches wide).

2 DETERMINE the dimensions to which you need to cut your fabric. For the base width, add the table width (36 inches), two drops (30 inches each), two puddles (6 inches each), and two seam allowances (½ inch each). Subtract two mitered band widths (27 inches each) from the total. Our total base width was 55 inches.
•For the base length, add the table length (96 inches), two drops (30 inches each), two puddles (6 inches each), and two seam allowances (½ inch each). Subtract two mitered band widths (27 inches each) from the total. Our total base length was 115 inches.
•For the length of the longer mitered bands, add your total base length (115 inches), two mitered band widths (27 inches each), and two allowances for the corners (3 inches each). Ours was 175 inches. Add 1 inch to the width for seam allowances (28 inches). Cut two lengths of fabric to these dimensions (175 inches x 28 inches).
•For the length of the shorter mitered bands, add your total base width (55 inches), two mitered band widths (27 inches each), and two allowances for the corners (3 inches each). Ours was 115 inches. Add 1 inch to the width for seam allowances (28 inches). Cut two lengths of fabric to these dimensions (115 inches x 28 inches).

3 DETERMINE the center of each of the four sides of the base by folding it alternately in half lengthwise and crosswise. Mark the center of each side with chalk. Determine the center of each mitered band by folding each one crosswise. Mark the center with chalk. Match the centers of the longer mitered bands to the longer sides of the base. Attach the pieces, pinning them together with right sides facing. Repeat the process with the shorter mitered bands and the ends of the base.
•Begin and end stitching (using either French seams or serging the seams) ½ inch from the corners of the base. Lay the fabric on a flat surface, and fold each corner to form a mitered point. Press folded corners. Pin at each crease, with right sides facing; then stitch along each crease from the base (catching the ½-inch gap you left) to the outer edges of each band. Trim excess fabric. Use pinking shears to trim the tablecloth's edge to the desired dimensions (ours is 108 inches x 168 inches).

STEP-BY-STEP
(LIGHT-BLUE HEMMED TABLECLOTH)

1 MEASURE the length, width, and drop of your table (ours is 3 feet wide and 8 feet long, with a 30-inch drop). Decide how much of a fabric puddle you prefer (ours is 6 inches). We used a doubled 6-inch hem.

2 DETERMINE the dimensions to which you need to cut your fabric. For the total width, add the table width (36 inches), two drops (30 inches each), two puddles (6 inches each), and four hems (6 inches each). Our total width is 132 inches. For the total length, add the table length (96 inches), two drops (30 inches each), two puddles (6 inches each), and four hems (6 inches each). For us, the total length is 192 inches.

3 CUT three pieces of fabric to your total length amount (we cut three 192-inch-long pieces). Sew lengthwise to connect all three widths with either French seams or serged seams.

4 TRIM the tablecloth to the total width measurement (ours is 132 inches), then fold the double hems. Topstitch the folded edge with matching thread, and press. (Note: Take care when pressing sheer fabrics; use low heat settings.)

NO-SEW TABLECLOTH FOR A ROUND TABLE

For a standard 60-inch round table, cut 4-yard-long pieces of three different-colored fabrics. Pink the fabric edges, and layer the three lengths on the table.

The glistening hues of gold, copper, and black in this no-sew tablecloth shimmer in the sunlight.

fine FABRICATIONS

With fabric and a little glue, you can quickly make an elegant tablecloth.

With just 1½ yards of fabric, you can make a handsome tablecloth like the one shown here. The square tablecloth is a versatile size that you can place diagonally on a round, square, or rectangular table. It requires no sewing; just hot-glue a double row of fringe around the edge of the fabric.

MAKE A NO-SEW TABLECLOTH

Select a heavy upholstery fabric that coordinates with the colors of your room. You'll need two types of fringe. Bullion fringe, measuring 4 to 6 inches long, is applied to the fabric first; it's followed by a tassel fringe that's glued on top of the bullion fringe.

Getting Started

TOOLS & MATERIALS
hot-glue gun and glue sticks
straight pins
1½ yards of 54-inch-wide fabric
6⅓ yards of bullion fringe
6⅓ yards of tassel fringe

1 BEGIN at the center of one side. Use the hot-glue gun to apply dots of glue near the edge of the fabric. Press the heading of the bullion fringe onto the glue. (If the glue comes through, don't touch it with your fingers. Instead, press the heading down with a folded washcloth.) At the corners of the fabric, fold the heading down at a 45-degree angle so that it will lie flat. Continue gluing the fringe in place until all four sides are covered.

2 APPLY dots of glue to the heading of the bullion fringe using the hot-glue gun. Press the heading of the tassel fringe onto the glue. Cover all four sides with the second row of fringe.

This opulent tablecloth was made by hot-gluing a double row of fringe to the edges of a square piece of upholstery fabric.

HANDMADE
for your TABLE

Change your table as easily as you change your mind with this reversible runner and matching napkins.

To help you make the best color and pattern selections for this project, take a piece of your china to the fabric store to use as a reference. Look for fabrics that repeat accent colors or contain designs that go with your china. Solid fabrics are also good, especially if there's a lot of pattern in your room. One quick tip to consider: If your china is partially cream or off-white, you should avoid a fabric that has a stark white background.

STEP-BY-STEP (TABLE RUNNER)

1 DETERMINE an appropriate length and width for your runner. With the table set, measure the length and width of the space between place settings; then add 1¼ inches (for two ⅝-inch seams) to each measurement. Convert the length to yards, and purchase an equivalent amount of yardage in each of the two fabrics you've chosen. (If your fabrics are at least 45 inches wide and you limit the width of the runner to about 20 inches, there will be enough fabric left for a few napkins.)

2 CUT each piece of fabric to the dimensions determined in Step 1. Pin fabric pieces together, right sides facing. Mark the center of each short side of fabric. To make the points, use a yardstick and tailor's chalk to measure and mark a line extending from the center of the short sides to each long side. Trim excess fabric by cutting along the chalk lines.

3 STITCH runner on sewing machine, using ⅝-inch seam allowance. With fabrics still pinned together, right sides facing, stitch down one long side, around both sides of 1 point, and up second long side. Press seams flat. Turn runner right side out, and press seams once again. On each side of unstitched point, turn ⅝-inch seam allowance to inside, and press. Then stitch opening by hand. Sew tassels to ends of runner. Remove the tassels before dry-cleaning the runner.

STEP-BY-STEP (NAPKINS)

1 CUT fabric to 21-inch squares (or as large as your remaining fabric permits). You can have the napkin edges serged (stitched in a way that binds them with thread) by a seamstress. Expect to pay about $1 to $2 per napkin. Or you can hem the napkins yourself by completing the following steps.

2 TURN ⅝ inch to wrong side along all four edges of one square of fabric; press to crease. Open creased folds; then turn each corner toward center, making a triangle. Trim off tip of each triangle.

3 MAKE hems by folding ¼ inch along each raw edge to wrong side; press. Fold again along first crease to form hem; pin. Hem with small slip stitches.

Getting Started

TOOLS & MATERIALS

yardstick	sewing machine
fabrics	thread
scissors	iron
straight pins	needle
tailor's chalk	tassels

EASY Burlap Tablecloth

An easy-to-make square overskirt adds texture and color to a plain skirted table.

Perk up a drab table with this simple-to-sew overskirt made of burlap and a colorful cotton fabric. You can find burlap in many colors for about $2.50 per yard. A medium-weight cotton or a similar weight fabric works best for the border. Purchase 1⅜ yards of burlap and 1½ yards of fabric for the border. Choose thread to match the border fabric and you'll have all the materials you need. The project costs less than $20, and it takes only a few hours of cutting and sewing. The finished size is 50 inches square, which fits over most side tables.

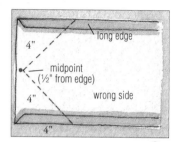

step 2

STEP-BY-STEP

1 TRIM burlap so length equals width. The finished size will be approximately 45 inches square. Set aside.

2 CUT four strips of border fabric 9 x 51 inches. Press ½ inch of long edges to wrong side. At the ends of each strip mark ½ inch in from midpoint. At each folded edge make a mark 4 inches from the end. Draw two lines connecting the marks to form a 90° angle. You may want to use a 90° triangle (or something square such as the corner of a magazine) to mark the angle.

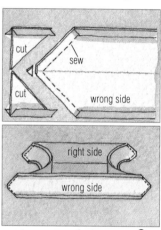

step 3

3 PIN the end of one strip to the end of a second strip (right sides together). Seam ends together following marked lines. Repeat to sew all four strips together and create one piece. Clip pointed edges. Press seams open. Turn right side out.

4 FOLD border in half (wrong sides together), aligning edges, and press to crease outer edge (border is 4 inches wide). Lay pressed border on a flat surface. Sandwich burlap edges between folds of border, and pin into place. Top-stitch through all layers 3⁄16 inch from inside border edge. Remove pins.

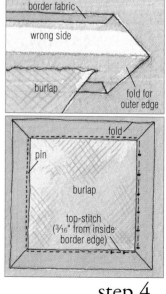

step 4

Getting Started

TOOLS & MATERIALS

1⅜ yards of 45-inch burlap

scissors

1½ yards of 36- to 45-inch border fabric

straight pins

thread to match border fabric

sewing machine

SKIRTED *and* SCALED

Fit a fabric-covered table into your decorating plan with these helpful tips.

A large table anchors this corner, providing plenty of display. Wide cording at the bottom of the skirt ensures a better drape.

SKIRT SMARTS

•You can use almost anything for the base—as long as it's sturdy and the right height. An old table, a wood crate, even heavy cardboard boxes work. For stability, the base should be as large as possible.

•Finished height should be between 24 and 29 inches (standard dining table height).

•The top can be cut from ¾-inch plywood or particle board. Some home-center stores offer ready-cut tops. Sand the edge and round it over to protect fabric.

•To calculate the size skirt needed, measure from the floor up to the top, across the top at its maximum width, and then down to the floor on the other side. If you want the skirt to puddle, add 2 to 3 inches.

•For the best drape, choose a medium to heavy fabric. Consider using a plain fabric for the skirt and then using a square of fabric as an overskirt. This will allow you to easily change the look.

Skirted tables offer easy and flexible alternatives to the usual end table. The round shape and draping fabric give them a softness not afforded by the hard edges of a rectangular wood piece.

For the best effect, a skirted table needs to be scaled to the room and to the other furniture. In the home of this Little Rock architect, a 45-inch-diameter table fills one corner of the den. "Big is the key," says the owner.

A smaller skirted table or even a rectangular end table might have room for a lamp, one picture, and perhaps a cup of coffee. But this table can accommodate all that and much more. "You can put a lot of stuff on them," he adds. "It's a focus for the room."

A large skirted table is also versatile. The 29-inch-high one pictured here, for example, can be pulled out and used for extra dining. At his previous home, this same table was used in the master bedroom, combined with two side chairs, for a casual spot for breakfast or use as a desk.

Another advantage of a skirted table, especially a large one, is the underneath storage space. Boxes of Christmas ornaments or other infrequently used items can be squirreled away, out of sight yet easily accessible.

DROP-LEAF TABLESCAPE

Simple suede can be embroidered to make luxurious leaves.

Layer the colors for a stunning display.

Y ou may grumble as you spend hours raking, but you've got to admire the sheer beauty of fall leaves. From sunny yellows to vivid reds to burnished browns, they provide the rich colors that the season often lacks in flowers.

To re-create these hues for an autumn table, we chose seven colors of soft washable suede, and then satin-stitched leaf shapes and veins. For a formal setting, we scattered the leaves to substitute for a table runner. On a more casual pine table, we used them as place mats. Linen napkins in a coordinating fabric complete the informal look.

STEP-BY-STEP (SUEDE LEAVES)

You'll need a basic sewing machine and lots of time for this project. Don't feel limited to oak leaves; branch out and sketch your own favorites.

1 USING the leaf pictured on the previous page as a guide, draw a leaf shape onto freezer paper. Our pattern measured approximately 20 inches long and 16 inches wide. Pin the leaf pattern onto the fabric, and cut out the shape.

2 FOLLOWING the manufacturer's directions, spray the wrong side of the leaf with temporary spray adhesive, and affix the wrong side of the fabric to the stabilizer.

3 FOR a satin stitch, use your machine's embroidery foot, and set the stitch width at 6 mm (or the maximum setting if your machine only goes to 5 mm). Set the stitch length to 0.25 or the satin-stitch option. Use the rayon thread in the needle and the multipurpose thread in the bobbin. Staying about ⅜ to ½ inch from the raw edge and beginning at the base, stitch the outline of the leaf. Remove stabilizer from the outer edges only.

4 USING your pattern as a guide, mark leaf veins directly onto fabric with a chalk marking pencil. Stitch along these lines, starting and ending your stitch width at 0. Stitch larger veins to a maximum width of 5 or 6 mm.

5 REMOVE remaining stabilizer. Carefully trim away the excess fabric next to the leaf outline stitching.

6 PRESS on the wrong side of the fabric. If necessary, wash to remove any remaining adhesive.

STEP-BY-STEP (NAPKINS)

1 CUT fabric into 18-inch squares. Fold ¾ inch to the front side, and press. Open out the edges; then fold each corner, aligning the creases. Press each diagonal fold. Open out corners. Fold at the center of the corner where the three creases meet. Align the raw edges; then stitch on the fold line. Trim the seam to ¼ inch, and press open. Turn the corner inside out. Make sure the point is sharp; then press. Repeat with each corner. Use rayon thread in the needle and multipurpose thread in the bobbin to topstitch along the edge of the ¾-inch allowance.

2 FOR each napkin, cut four strips of tear-away stabilizer about 2 inches wide and the length of the napkin. Using temporary spray adhesive, affix the strips to the back side of the napkin, aligning edges. Cut water-soluble stabilizer into 1-inch-wide strips. Center transparent strips over topstitched line.

3 SET up your machine as you did for the leaves. Satin-stitch over the strips and the topstitched line, pivoting at the mitered corners. Using this extra layer of stabilizer results in a smoother finish for the satin stitch.

4 REMOVE all excess stabilizer. Press. If necessary, wash to remove any remaining adhesive.

Napkins in jute-colored linen add fall color to the table. The satin-stitched edges echo the outlines and contours of the leaves.

RUSTIC GOOD LOOKS

Treat your table to a helping of color and style with one simple table decoration that can work for two looks.

The perfect tablecloth and place mats can be hard to find in the color and pattern that you want, especially if you have an odd-size table or limited budget. Instead of purchasing a cloth and mats, look for reasonably priced fabrics in the colors you want. The next step is to figure out how to use all the colors at once.

We selected a fabric and created three different panels (the same size) to drape across the table. A fourth panel was made to stretch the length of the table. Besides working well for a seated gathering (see page 73), the fabrics can also be knotted together for use as a runner (see below and on facing page).

STEP-BY-STEP (FABRIC PANELS)

1 MEASURE the table length and width to determine panel measurements. The table length sets the tone for the number to be seated and for one panel that runs under the crosswise panels. The width of the crosswise panels equals a standard place mat, no more than 18 inches. Their length should be the width of the table plus the amount of drop length for each side. (Our drop is 9 inches. This times 2 plus a 34-inch table width equals a total finished length of 52 inches.) Determine which color is suitable for the long panel, if assorted colors are used.

2 WORKING on the reverse side, prepare each panel of fabric by folding it lengthwise so that when cut, a top and bottom panel is formed. Keep in mind, the folded side seam will remain intact. Using the folded edge as one of the sides, measure panel width and length, adding a 1-inch seam allowance. Mark measurements with pins or fabric pencil.

3 CUT out the panels, maintaining the folded side piece, and pin into place.

4 KEEPING the fabric inside out, sew the three cut edges of the panel, leaving several inches open at the end. Cut excess fabric from each corner at a diagonal, so corners lie smooth once finished. Turn fabric right side out through the opening. Hand-sew the opening closed.

5 ARRANGE the panel so the seam is centered on the underside; press panel flat. Repeat with each additional panel. Tie a tassel (see instructions below) to each end of the long panel to complete.

STEP-BY-STEP (TASSELS)

1 CUT small strips out of scrap fabric, keeping some ends frayed.

2 STUFF a paper cup with tissue so it feels solid. Place strips over it using alternate colors. Place a rubber band around the cup, securing the strips.

3 COVER the paper cup by wrapping it with a rectangular piece of fabric to form the tassel's top. Glue the fabric to the cup and ribbons under the lower edge of the fabric and along the side to complete the body.

4 GLUE on trim to conceal raw edges. Add ribbon or cording for a tie at the top, and close with a final piece of trim.

step 1   step 2   step 3   step 4

Four easily constructed panels are used in lieu of a tablecloth and place mats. There were no hems to finish, no table round to piece together, and no complicated measuring.

73

GOOD *Impressions*

*Use rubber stamps to print designs on fabric—bold accents
of color are an attractive option.*

Large rubber stamps are available at art-supply stores for imprinting decorative patterns on fabric, wood, paper, and other surfaces. With the stamps, you can create designs on cocktail and dinner napkins and then add accents of colorful fabric paint. You'll find stamps for printing the sun, moon, and stars, as well as animal and botanical motifs. They're priced at approximately $5 to $8 each.

Because natural fibers absorb the ink and paint used for this project, napkins made of cotton or linen work best. The first step is to wash, starch, and iron your napkins and a piece of practice fabric; this will remove sizing and create a crisp, yet absorbent, finish.

Practice imprinting designs and painting colors on the extra fabric or napkin. Once you're able to achieve consistent results, you're ready to decorate the napkins.

1 PLACE a tablespoon of ink on the glass. With the brayer, roll the ink onto an area measuring about 4 x 6 inches.

2 CENTER the stamp on the inked glass, and press it into the ink.

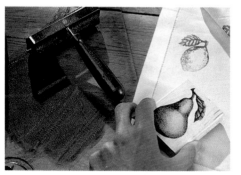

3 PRESS the inked stamp onto the napkin, and pull the stamp straight up. If the ink builds up on the stamp after several uses, rinse it with water. When you're finished, rinse the glass, brayer, and rubber stamp.

4 LET the ink dry. You can brush on a colored border of fabric paint and fill in the imprinted design with color. Check ink and paint manufacturer's instructions for tips on using an iron to heat-set the designs, making them waterproof.

Getting Started

TOOLS & MATERIALS
piece of glass measuring approximately 10 x 12 inches

cotton or linen napkins

extra fabric for practice

From an art supply store:
large rubber stamps

small rubber brayer

jar of water-base, black screen-printing ink

bottles of water-base permanent fabric paint

½-inch-wide artist's watercolor paintbrush

IDEAS THAT WORK
•Kitchen-supply catalogs are a good source of linen and cotton napkins that are both affordable and well made.

•Imprint a single design in one corner or stamp several different shapes around the edge of the napkin.

MIXED VEGETABLES

Easy-to-make stamps create fun designs on a tablecloth.

All it takes is a big serving of hand-painted vegetables to create your own colorful tablecloth.

The tablecloth itself requires no sewing to assemble. For a 26- to 30-inch-diameter round table, use 1½ yards of 54-inch-wide canvas. Fold over a 1-inch hem on all sides, and seal with washable fabric glue.

Use compressed sponges from an art-supply store to make a variety of vegetable stamps from the patterns found on pages 78-79. The sponges are thin and easy to cut with scissors. Once the stamps are made, simply dip them into the paint, and press onto the fabric.

If you choose to paint a purchased tablecloth instead of making your own, be sure to opt for one composed of natural fibers. An all-cotton fabric is preferable to a synthetic one because it will absorb paint better.

STEP-BY-STEP

1 PURCHASE or assemble a tablecloth. To make your own, cut the shape from canvas, and finish the ends with a 1-inch hem held in place with washable fabric glue.

2 USE a copy machine to copy the vegetable patterns to the desired size. Then trace the patterns onto tracing paper, and cut them out. Transfer shapes onto compressed sponges, and cut them out.

3 WET the sponges and squeeze dry. Pour acrylic paint on a disposable plate. If the paint is too thick, thin it with textile medium. Dip a sponge into the paint; press it onto the tablecloth. With a paintbrush, add highlights and shadows to the vegetables on the tablecloth using different paint shades. Create a checkered border around the tablecloth with a small square sponge.

step 2

step 3

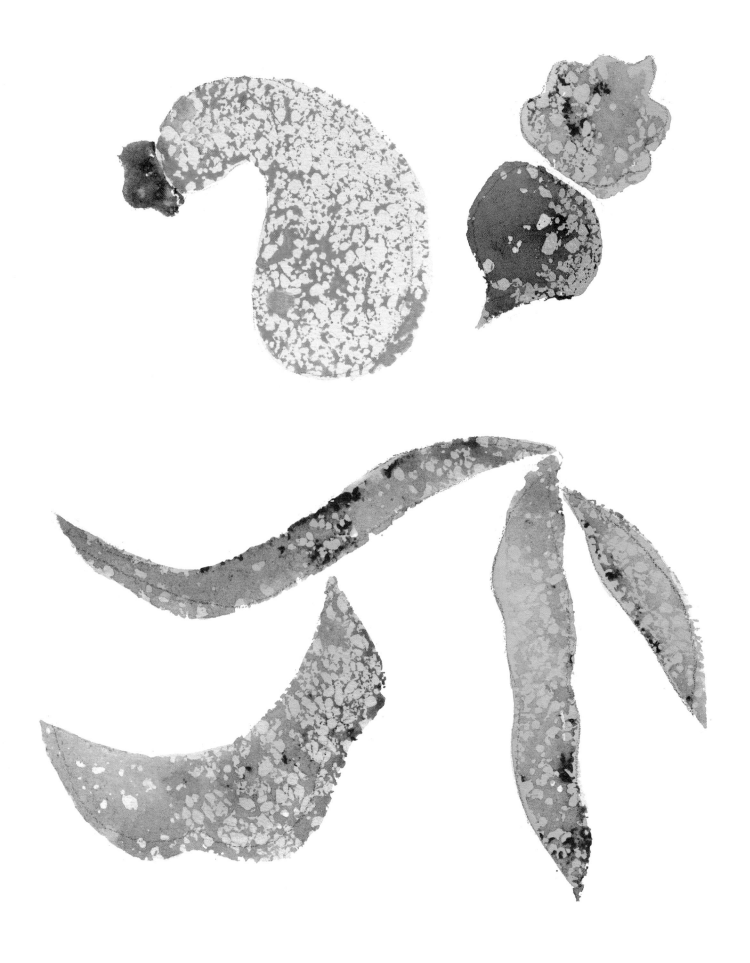

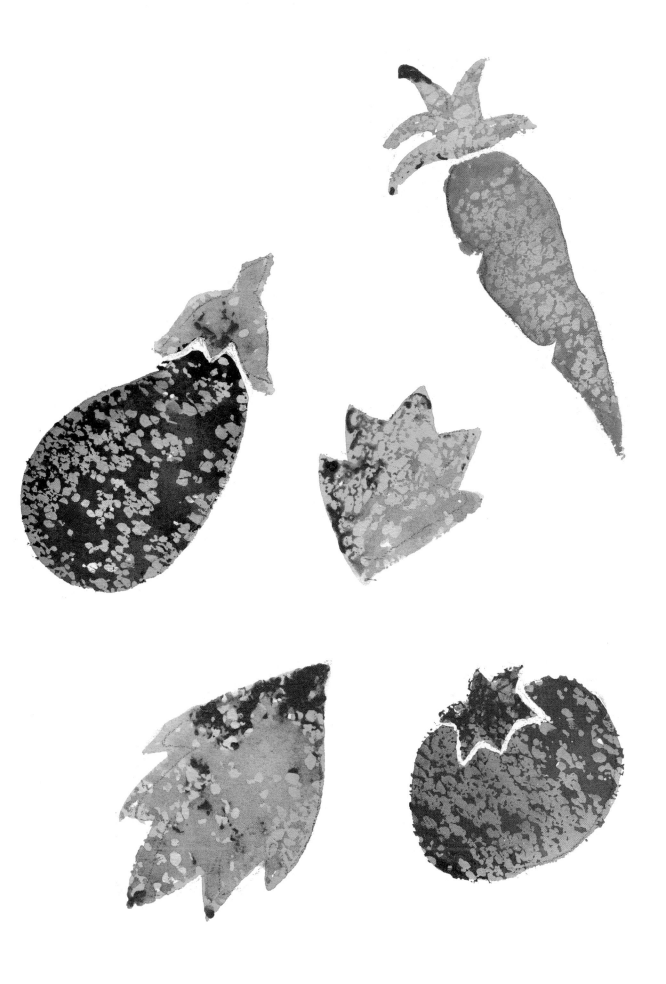

STAMP ACT

Add a festive touch to a table covering with metallic imprints in various shapes.

With this easy and inexpensive stamping technique, you can create an antique-looking table square made of painted velvet. Despite its elegant look, the table topper is made from affordable materials. You can adapt this technique for decorating many other materials and surfaces.

We used florist foam—the dry, spongy material used in flower arranging—for the stamps, because the lightweight foam is easy to cut and holds its shape well. Whittling a leaf-shaped stamp from florist foam took us about 30 seconds; dipping the stamp into paint and imprinting a pattern of leaves took about a minute and looked surprisingly good. Outlining a 2-inch-wide space with tape and filling it in with bronze spray paint resulted in a strip of sheer color resembling metallic ribbon. By dipping stamps in gold paint and pressing them onto the bronze area, detail and depth were easy to achieve. Dots and dashes of contrasting paints were applied with brushes to accent the other designs.

This method of painting fabric is fun, and it quickly gives ordinary upholstery velvet an aged look. From a single block of florist foam costing less than $2, you can easily make a dozen or more reusable stamps of various sizes—enough to embellish writing paper, walls, wooden trays, boxes, and numerous other surfaces.

STEP-BY-STEP (STAMPING FABRIC)

1 USE a copy machine to enlarge the shapes on opposite page to the desired sizes. Cut out the shapes from paper. Cut a 2- or 2½-inch-thick slice from florist foam. (Use a kitchen knife or draw a piece of monofilament fishing line through the foam.) Using the pattern, draw a shape on a smooth side of the florist foam. With a craft knife, cut the shape at least 1 inch deep into the block of foam. Start at the sides, cutting away enough foam to make the shape extend at least an inch. Repeat for other shapes.

2 USE a yardstick and pencil or ballpoint pen to outline a band of velvet fabric approximately 2 inches from each edge. The band can be ½ inch to 2 inches or more in width. Outline the band by applying a strip of masking tape to each edge. Hold the nozzle of the spray paint can approximately 2 inches from the taped areas, and apply the paint.

3 POUR metallic paint onto a plate or a disposable palette. Dip the stamp into the paint, and press it onto the fabric to create a line of shapes located on or near the spray-painted band. Blend a little water or textile medium into the paint if it's difficult to apply. Accent these painted areas by brushing on contrasting metallic paint in repetitive patterns, such as slashes, dots, or dashes. Continue applying spray-painted bands in various widths, as well as stamping more designs and hand painting additional accents.

STEP-BY-STEP (FINISHING THE TABLE SQUARE)

1 TRIM the selvages from the painted fabric and lining. Place lining (right side up) on work surface. Place painted velvet (wrong side up) on top of lining. Align one of the trimmed selvage edges of both pieces of fabric. (You may need to trim one or the other fabric pieces to make them perfectly square.) Place a drinking glass at each corner, and trim both pieces of fabric. Separate fabrics.

Getting Started

TOOLS & MATERIALS

For stamping fabric:

block of florist foam

kitchen knife or monofilament fishing line

pencil

sharp craft knife

yardstick

ballpoint pen

1½ yards upholstery velvet

masking tape

spray enamel in colors such as gold, copper, and bronze

plate or palette

paintbrushes

metallic acrylic craft paint in gold, copper, and bronze

textile medium

For making table square:

scissors

1½ yards of 54-inch-wide lining fabric

painted velvet

drinking glasses

straight pins

6½ yards flanged cording

sewing machine with zipper foot

needle and thread

iron

2 PIN flange of cording to edge of velvet on painted side. (Cording should turn toward center; flange should touch cut fabric edge.) Where ends of cording cross, pin them outside the seam allowance. With the zipper foot on the sewing machine, stitch cording to fabric, placing stitching near cording.

3 BASTE painted fabric and lining together, right sides facing. Machine-stitch along previous stitching line, leaving a 12-inch opening. Turn table square inside out, stitch opening closed, and press.

GOING
Undercover

Whether it's to change with the seasons or to hide an old piece that's seen better days, slipcovering furniture is one of the most instantly gratifying ways to change the look of your home. You're sure to be inspired by the many options we show here.

First we arranged the slipcover on the sofa; then we finished by sewing fabric-covered buttons on to hold a tab, which pulls the cover smooth across the front and sides.

REFRESHER COURSE

Long favored for their relaxed good looks, slipcovers are an easy way to add new personality to tired furnishings.

The hand-me-down sofa. The mail-order coffee table. The yard sale bargain chairs. The seen-better-days end table. We're all familiar with the staples of a first apartment. But when these gems start to lose their bohemian charm, consider covering rather than tossing them. A few yards of fabric can pull those post-college questionables into a sophisticated, grown-up look that still fits in a macaroni-and-cheese budget.

SLIPCOVERS

A slipcover is a perfect way to bring a worn sofa into style and extend its life. We chose an easy, do-it-yourself version for this large sofa. It's basically a large rectangle of fabric that requires little more than knowing how to sew a seam. Patterns with measuring instructions are available in fabric stores.

To give our simple cover a more dressed-up look, we constructed it in a green washed linen and hired a workroom to make one long back pillow in a beautiful toile fabric. The insert is a feather-and-down body pillow, which can be found in some home or bedding stores. Additional throw pillows are green linen with a luxurious silk border in a check pattern.

Tailored seat covers hide mismatched needlepoint seats on armchairs found at a yard sale. The formal air they provide helps elevate the room as a whole.

TABLE COVERS

This mail-order coffee table with an iron base and wood top is useful but doesn't have a lot of personality. A length of toile fabric gives it a quick and attractive face-lift. Cut a piece large enough to cover the top and wrap around the sides. Cut a second piece of plain cotton fabric to use as a liner between the wood and toile. Then simply pull the two layers tight around the table, and use a staple gun to secure the fabric to the underside of the wood top. A piece of ¼-inch glass protects the fabric.

IDEAS THAT WORK

•Remove the sofa's back cushions, and mass a variety of throw pillows along the back, on top of the slipcover. Cover the pillows in one fabric or a variety of complementary patterns.

•Sew fitted covers in a coordinating fabric for the bottom cushions, and set them on top of the slipcover. This keeps the slipcover from shifting and pulling out of place.

•Add a wide border of contrasting fabric or trim around the edge of the slipcover. Repeat the fabric or trim on throw pillows.

A quality fabric elevates an ordinary mail-order coffee table.

A QUICK COVER-UP

A simple painter's cloth gives a handsome new look to an old sofa.

Need a really fast fix for a dated sofa? One that won't cost a fortune? Don't reupholster it. Try covering your sofa with a painter's drop cloth instead.

You can find cotton canvas drop cloths at most paint stores. The largest size, 12 x 15 feet, runs about $50 and is ideal for a full-size sofa. You will also need cording or sisal rope to hold the canvas in place. Coordinating tassels are optional.

Leave the back pillows in place while covering the sofa, or remove them and arrange accent pillows over the drop cloth.

STEP-BY-STEP

1 REMOVE the back pillows from the sofa if you plan to add accent pillows. Drape the canvas over the sofa, centering the fabric from side to side. Allow a few extra inches in front, and turn under. Tuck fabric between seat cushions, along the back, and on both sides. Pull excess to the back, and turn under.

2 MEASURE the length and width of the sofa, and multiply by 2 to determine the amount of cording or rope needed. (You may want to double the measurement and twist the two lengths together.) Wrap cording around bottom of sofa, and knot in the back. Measure around the arm, and cut one piece of cording for each arm. Wrap cording around and over each arm, tie ends together, and tuck cording between the seat cushion and the sides of the sofa.

3 TIE tassels to the cording around the arms. Arrange pillows across the back.

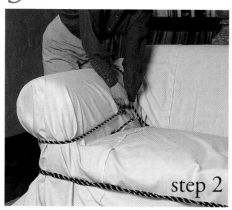

step 2

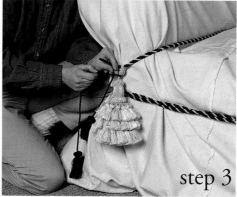

step 3

Needlepoint pillows in muted tones cover the back of the sofa for a perfect finishing touch. Fluffy tassels and thick cording add rich details.

before

LIGHTEN UP

An easy way to brighten your room is to slipcover the chairs.
With this no-sew technique, you'll have your chairs covered in
an afternoon!

When warm weather arrives, freshen the seating in your home by shifting into neutrals. Neutral slipcovers, that is. Using inexpensive canvas drop cloths as a source of fabric, you can adapt these quick ideas for covering both wooden dining chairs and upholstered arm chairs. Finish off the fabric edges the no-sew way, using both iron-on Stitch Witchery and a hot-glue gun. For a custom finishing touch, use fabric paint to create a colorful border on the bottom edge of the slipcover. Choose jazzy accent pillows to complete the new look.

The easy dining chair covers each consist of two panels. One is laid across the chair seat from side to side. The other is placed on the chair from front to back. Fabric ties attached to each panel hold the chair covers in place.

Transform an upholstered chair by covering it with a canvas drop cloth; use one edge of the drop cloth to form the lower front edge of the chair cover. Tuck in the drop cloth around the seat and back cushions. (You may need to cut off excess fabric in the back.) To add a decorative touch, use fabric paint to create a checked pattern along the bottom edge of the slipcover.

STEP-BY-STEP (DINING CHAIR SLIPCOVERS)

1 CUT a piece of canvas that is 2 inches wider and longer than the width and length of the chair. (Measure the length of the slipcover from the back of the chair starting at the floor to the front of the chair ending at the floor.) Cut your next piece of canvas 2 inches wider and longer measuring from floor side to floor side over the seat. The extra 2 inches are used to form a hem.

2 USING Stitch Witchery and a warm iron, form a 1-inch hem on each of the four sides of your two pieces of canvas.

3 CUT 16 (8- x 1-inch) pieces of canvas to create ties. Place an 8-inch piece of Stitch Witchery in the center of one piece of cut canvas. Fold the two canvas edges over the Stitch Witchery and warm with an iron. Repeat for remaining 15 pieces.

4 PLACE cut slipcover pieces on chair to mark where the ties need to be glued to hold the covers together. (We glued eight ties on the top and eight on the bottom.)

5 USING a hot-glue gun, attach 2 inches of a tie to your marking. Repeat for all ties.

6 TIE the pieces of canvas together in square knots.

7 REPEAT steps 1 through 6 for the number of chairs you want to cover.

Inexpensive canvas drop cloths make great-looking slipcovers.

Getting Started

TOOLS & MATERIALS

scissors

2 (9- x 12-foot) canvas drop cloths

5 Stitch Witchery packets
(regular weight)

iron

hot-glue gun and glue sticks

ALL *dressed* UP

Give five wooden chairs different looks using one pattern.

Many manufacturers of dress patterns also offer craft patterns for making window treatments, pillow covers, tablecloths, and many other items for the home. They are found in fabric stores and often contain instructions for making several versions of one item. We used Simplicity pattern #9452 for chair seat covers to transform each of these five chairs. By choosing from several skirt styles, adjusting the skirt length, varying the fabric, and stitching interesting ties, you can create a custom look. It isn't difficult to modify a basic pattern. For variations on this pattern, lengthen or shorten a skirt, omit pleats, or add a scalloped edge.

When designing a seat cover, consider the chair's features and surroundings. For a tailored look, choose a pleated skirt. For a softer, more graceful appearance, try a gathered skirt. Play up interesting characteristics such as a chair's scalloped edge. Decide on a complementary skirt length. Use long skirts to hide worn chair legs, or short skirts to reveal legs with pleasing detail.

Fabric color and design are also important. Lightweight fabrics such as gingham, broadcloth, chintz, cotton, or cotton blends work best. Choose a floral chintz for a dressy look or gingham for a casual style.

Tassels in all colors and styles are available at upholstery fabric shops. Use 3- or 4-inch-wide ties to make bows, or try decorative ribbon.

Breathe new life into old wooden chairs with these simple seat covers. Select a variety of styles, lengths, and fabrics to accent any room. Add decorative ties and tassels for the perfect finishing touch.

A bright floral skirt with green piping perks up a modest furniture piece.

A long skirt and large tassel ties create soft elegance.

The skirt's scalloped hem repeats a detail on the wooden chair. To create the scalloped edging, use a cup as a guide for outlining scallops on brown kraft paper. Cut out the scallops, and use the paper template when cutting fabric for the edge of the skirt.

Garden-inspired fabric and moss-colored bows yield a crisp look.

Give character to a forgotten corner with a painted chair covered in plaid material.

Chair Seat
COVER STORY

Less than a yard of fabric, a piece of muslin, and a

staple gun are all you need to re-cover a seat.

Getting Started

TOOLS & MATERIALS

For a pair of chair seats:

paper for pattern (paper must be larger than chair seat)

⅔ yard 54-inch-wide fabric (more may be needed to center a design)

muslin or black cloth

staple gun and staples

The essence of good decorating is in the details. And one of the easiest details to update is a seat covering. Whether you cover a set of dining chairs or a bench, a minimal amount of fabric can have maximum impact on a room. Select durable fabrics that will wear well and coordinate with existing upholstery. With the help of a staple gun, you can transform your chair seat or bench in a snap.

STEP-BY-STEP

1 TURN the chair over, and remove corner screws and chair seat. (An electric screwdriver will be helpful.) Place seat on a large piece of paper, and cut a pattern that is 3 inches larger on all sides.

2 CENTER the chair seat pattern on the fabric, and cut around the pattern. Remove the pattern, and center the chair seat upside down on the wrong side of the cut fabric.

3 PULL excess fabric to the back, and staple it to secure. Begin stapling at the center of each side, and gradually work toward the corners.

4 PULL excess fabric toward center of seat at corners. Smooth and fold down fabric before stapling.

5 CUT a piece of muslin or black cloth that is the same size as the chair seat. Turn edges under, and staple to bottom of the chair seat, covering the raw edges of the fabric.

6 REPLACE seat on the chair, and insert the screws through holes on the underside.

One of the easiest details to change in a room is a chair's seat covering.

Re-covering this bench's removable seat with new fabric adds an instant update to the room's decor. Accent pillows in the same fabric reinforce the design.

BIG LOOK, simple steps

You'll be propping your feet up before you know it with this easy ottoman project.

The lowly footstool has been steadily moving up in the world. Now popularly referred to as an ottoman, this oh-so-mobile piece of furniture touts many forms and functions. Treat it as a coffee table, a cocktail table, a side table, a casual dinner-on-the-floor table. Glide it over to the fireplace as a cozy seat for two. Use its level surface for playing board games or piecing a puzzle. And by all means, slide it up to the sofa, love seat, or club chair, to elevate your feet.

This fun-to-place furnishing is fun to make too. We've provided a simple version using plywood, foam, and prefabricated wooden feet. We've also included instructions for a slipcover, which makes it easy to keep your ottoman clean and to give it a fresh look.

Buy the plywood and wooden feet at a home-supply store; purchase the foam, muslin, batting, slipcover fabric, and thread at an upholstery fabric store. You'll also need a staple gun, a drill, and maybe a pad and pencil to list all the other ottoman uses you'll dream up while putting it together.

STEP-BY-STEP (OTTOMAN)

1 APPLY walnut stain to prefabricated legs following manufacturer's instructions. Seal with a coat of paste wax or clear varnish. Set aside to dry. On the plywood, mark drill holes for the legs 2½ inches in from each side at the four corners. Drill a clearance hole for the blind-mounting nuts (T-nuts). Insert the nuts by tapping in with a hammer. (The prongs hold the nut in place and provide threaded inserts for the leg screw.) Screw legs into the blind-mounting nuts.

2 CUT batting to 36 x 48 inches, and lay flat on a clean surface. Place foam in middle of batting. Position plywood base with feet upside down on foam. Pull batting to underside of plywood, and staple in place, attaching the middle of each side first then working your way to the corners. Fold corners neatly, and pull batting taut.

3 CUT muslin fabric to 36 x 48 inches; press. Lay flat on a clean surface. Position ottoman on muslin, and repeat stapling process above.

STEP-BY-STEP (SLIPCOVER)

1 CUT slipcover fabric to 36 x 48 inches, and press. Cut 8½-inch squares from all four corners. Turn all edges under ½ inch, and press. Then turn edges under 1 inch, and press for hem. Stitch in place by hand or with a machine. Reinforce corner points with several hand stitches.

2 CUT 8 strips of fabric to 1½ x 13 inches for ties. The finished size will be ½ x 13 inches. Press one short end under ⅛ inch. Press in half lengthwise (wrong sides together), turning raw edges into the middle. Stitch close to the folded edge. Repeat to complete all 8 strips. Machine- or hand-stitch each tie to inside of slipcover 2 inches down from corner point. Place slipcover on ottoman, and tie bows at each corner.

This multiuse, do-it-yourself ottoman, with its prefabricated feet, may open the day as a coffee table and close it as a fireside bench.

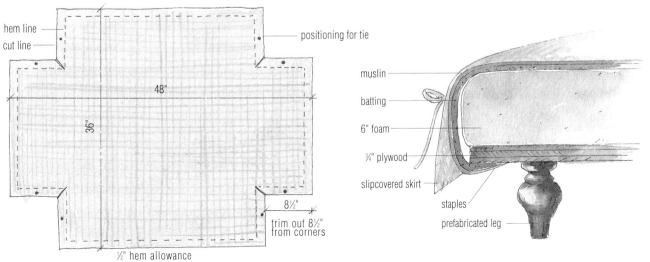

hem line

cut line

positioning for tie

48"

36"

8½"

trim out 8½" from corners

½" hem allowance

muslin

batting

6" foam

¾" plywood

slipcovered skirt

staples

prefabricated leg

PILLOW TALK

As a design accent they can't be topped. Available in every conceivable shape and size, pillows are the quick fix for every home decorator. From plain to fancy, our showcase of comfortable cushions is sure to please.

PILLOWS *with* PERSONALITY

Good pillows bring color, texture, and pattern to your rooms, while enhancing comfort and livability.

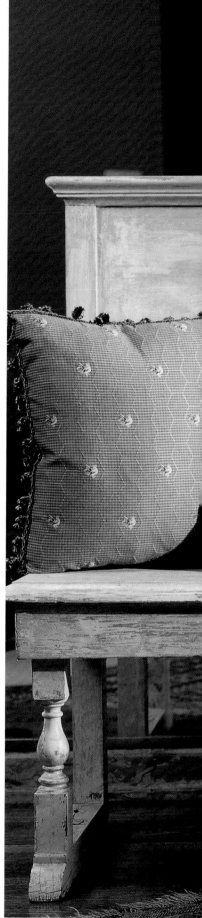

There's scarcely an accent or accessory that offers more decorative options than a handsome pillow. "Pillows give you a chance to indulge in more beautiful fabrics and more exquisite trims than you might be able to use for your draperies and upholstery," says designer Lou Alice Rogers of Nashville.

"Not everybody feels comfortable being adventurous with their paint colors or sofa fabrics," she says. "But pillows—now there's a place you can give in to your whims. I like a little splash, even in the most formal spaces."

Lou Alice doesn't believe that everything must match for a room to look coordinated. "I'm convinced that pillows do their best work when they don't match the walls and curtains perfectly. Why buy a pillow that's going to fade into your sofa? Smart pillows are accent pieces, not part of an outfit," she notes. "They're an inexpensive way to add depth to a decorating scheme: new colors, varied textures, rich patterns, and even a little story with some fabrics."

Her own beautifully made designs combine touchable fabrics with exciting fringes, tassels, and trims. They also provide a way to transform a room. "You may not be able to swap out your furniture from season to season," says Lou Alice, "but you can swap out your pillows for a whole new mood. Cool linens in fun shapes can bring a summery lightness to a room; in the cooler months you can cozy up the same room with pillows in rich fall tones and luscious trims." Have confidence in your own taste, and let your imagination shine through.

PILLOW POINTERS

•Consider the upholstery fabrics. If a sofa has a large pattern, choose pillows with a small repeat, perhaps with a coordinating, multihued trim that will pull in as many shades as possible. If your sofa is subdued in tone or upholstered in a small pattern, add texture and depth by using an interesting combination of fabrics and trims.

•Compare the size of the pillow to the furniture piece. A 20-inch pillow almost fills the back of most upholstered armchairs. Choose one measuring 16 inches square or 12 x 16 inches for a less overstuffed, more understated look.

ELEGANT STENCILING

Accessorize with hand-painted pillows— they're fun and affordable.

It's easy to add color, pattern, and personality to a chair or sofa using a pillow you've stenciled. You can create stencils for leaves, stars, and sunbursts with the patterns on pages 104-105. A copier will give you the flexibility of enlarging and reducing these shapes before you trace them onto acetate. By making stencils in several sizes, you'll have many more decorating options. Or let the designs on these pages inspire you to create your own designs.

You'll find that it's very easy to make a stencil, paint the fabric, and then sew a quick pillow cover. Or if you prefer, you can stencil designs directly onto a ready-made pillow.

STEP-BY-STEP

1 PLACE a piece of acetate over one of the stencil patterns, and trace the design with a pencil or ballpoint pen. Before cutting, be sure to protect the work surface with cardboard. Use a craft knife to cut away the outlined shapes.

2 POSITION the stencil on the fabric. Use the gold paint marker to fill in the shapes. Although dry cleaning is recommended for home-furnishing fabrics, it may cause the stenciling to fade. In that case, just use the paint marker to retouch the stenciling. If you prefer, use gold fabric paint instead of the gold paint marker. Use a stencil brush to dab paint through openings in the stencil. When the paint is dry, follow paint manufacturer's instructions for heat-setting the paint. Items decorated with fabric paint may be washed, but should not be dry-cleaned unless recommended by the paint manufacturer.

3 CUT two squares of fabric that measure 17¼ inches x 17¼ inches each for a pillow measuring approximately 16 x 16 inches. On the right side of one piece of fabric, use a pencil to lightly mark a seam line ⅝ inch from edges. Match the heading (the tape at the top of the fringe) to the seam line, and hand baste it in place. (The fringe should turn toward the center of the fabric.) Machine-stitch the fringe to the fabric, stitching at the base of the heading. Remove basting threads. Pin the squares of fabric together, right sides facing. Turn the fabric over so that the stitching is visible. Machine-stitch over the previous row of stitching, leaving a 12-inch opening at the bottom of the pillow cover. Clip excess fabric at corners of the pillow cover and turn it right side out. Fill the pillow cover with polyester batting, or insert a soft pillow form. To close the pillow opening, stitch it by hand.

Getting Started

TOOLS & MATERIALS

For stencils:
sheet of opaque acetate

craft knife

gold opaque oil-base paint marker or gold fabric paint and stencil brush

For each 16- x 16-inch pillow cover:

1 yard of 45- or 54-inch-wide polished-cotton fabric

thread

2½ yards fringe

polyester batting or 16- x 16-inch down-filled pillow form or another type of soft pillow form (or ready-made pillows)

Trace our pattern onto acetate, and cut out shapes with a craft knife. Use a paint marker (or fabric paint and brush) to stencil the design onto fabric.

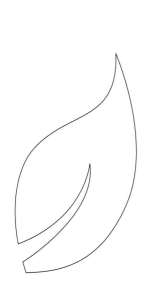

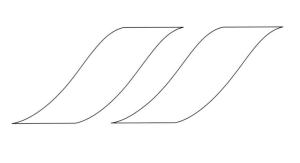

PAINTED CUSHIONS

Vibrant custom-designed pillows enliven the chairs in this breakfast room.

To decorate a room, start with your favorite things, such as the room's color scheme or existing accessories, and build on that. The accent colors in this kitchen were inspired by a tile design. To incorporate its pattern and bright hues in the breakfast area, seat cushions were painted for a touch of personal style.

Designs can be painted on premade cushions; however, the project is much easier if cotton duck fabric is purchased by the yard first, measured to fit your chair, and then painted before the cushion is constructed. Keep in mind that basic designs in geometric shapes are easier to duplicate.

STEP-BY-STEP

1 USE a copy machine to enlarge the design to the desired size. Another option is to simply use a stencil or stamp for your pattern. You can then skip to Step 3.

2 TRANSFER the pattern onto tracing paper with a fabric pencil or iron-on marker. Iron pattern onto cushions. (Note: This can be tricky with prefinished cushions due to lack of support on the underside.)

3 TAPE off any areas where paint is not supposed to go. Fill in the design with acrylic paint in your choice of colors. (Tip: Buy a small artist's canvas to sample different hues before you start. This will show how the paint will look when dry.) To create the side stripes, tape off every other inch, and paint between tape strips.

Getting Started

TOOLS & MATERIALS

100% cotton premade cushions or fabric to make cushions

tracing paper from a crafts or fabric store

fabric pencil or iron-on marker (If applied properly, marks should disappear within days.)

masking tape

acrylic or fabric paint

paintbrushes

stencils or stamps (optional)

step 2

step 3

STRONG *on* CHARM

Brightly colored canvas is a great start for comfy, durable pillows.

I t's referred to as cotton duck, canvas, sailcloth, or drop cloth. It's been around for years and has been used in many ways because of its strength. Today, designers are taking advantage of this great cloth to add informality and comfort to the home.

This heavyweight fabric comes in solids and stripes. It's perfect for outdoor pillows to cheer up plain furniture. And not only is the fabric durable, but it's also affordable and washable.

Before starting a project, be sure to prewash the fabric, dry on high heat, and use a heavy-duty needle in your sewing machine. Using these instructions, you can sew pillow covers in just a few hours. You can find all you need—colored canvas, matching thread, snap tape, and a 14-inch pillow form at the fabric store.

STEP-BY-STEP

1 CUT two pieces of each canvas, 14 inches x 15½ inches. Fold one edge of the 15½-inch side to the inside ½ inch, and press. Pin strip of snap tape to the right side ⅛ inch from fold, and stitch in place. Repeat process on the second square, lining up the mate side of the snap tape. Fold each snap edge over 1 inch, and press (so that snap tape is in middle of folds).

2 PLACE right sides together, folds in place and snaps facing out, and pin together. Stitch a ½-inch seam on three sides. Secure the stitching at snap opening with several backstitches. Turn right side out. Insert pillow form, and snap together.

step 2

Bathing Beauties

Take a casual attitude and sew terry cloth
pillows in playful colors.

Ideal for waterside furniture, terry cloth is an inexpensive washable fabric perfect for colorful pillows and cushion covers. Include different shapes and sizes for interest, and make a few oversize pillows for the floor.

STEP-BY-STEP (BEACH BALL)

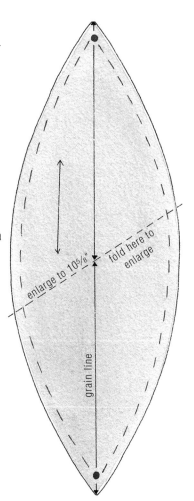

1 ENLARGE pattern piece on a copier to measure 21¼ inches long. (Copy each half of the pattern to measure 10⅝ inches.) Tape the halves together to make your pattern. Cut out six pieces of fabric, each a different color, and mark dots at both ends on wrong side of fabric. Stay-stitch ¼ inch around edges of each piece.

2 ALIGN two pieces, pin right sides together, and machine-stitch a ½-inch seam between dots. Backstitch at each dot. (Stopping at the dots is critical.) Repeat, adding each additional section to form the ball cover. On last section, leave a 5-inch opening.

3 STUFF with Fiberfil until desired fullness is reached, and slip-stitch closed.

4 PURCHASE three shells with holes in them, or drill small holes with a high-speed hobby drill such as a Dremel Moto-Tool. Use small cording in three different lengths. String a piece of cord through hole in each shell, and knot on the underside of the shell. Tie the three pieces of cord together in a knot, and attach to beach ball with needle and thread.

STEP-BY-STEP (SWING SEAT)

1 CUT one piece of each of the four fabrics 46 x 15 inches, which includes a ⅝-inch seam allowance. Stay-stitch ½ inch from edge around all sides. (Finished pillow size is 55 x 22 inches, which fits a standard swing seat.)

2 ALIGN two pieces of fabric along the 46-inch sides, and pin right sides together. Machine-stitch using a ⅝-inch seam. Zigzag along each side of seam to prevent raveling. Repeat to join all four panels. Fold out seams, and press.

3 FOLD sewn panels in half, with right sides together, across the width. Align ends, and pin into place. Machine-stitch 1 inch from edge along the two outer panels only. Leave the two center panels open to insert self-fastening strips. Machine-stitch short ends using a ⅝-inch seam allowance. Curve seam in slightly at fold (front corners) to prevent pointed ends. Trim seam allowances at corners.

4 PIN and machine-stitch each piece of self-fastening strips to each side of fabric opening in seam allowance. (Stitch to the right side of fabric.) Turn cover right side out. Fold seam allowance to inside; topstitch strips. Do this for both sides of opening. Smooth each corner, and insert pillow forms. Fasten self-fastening strips.

Warm up a wood bench with pillows made from a man's cotton pullover and a lady's wool cardigan.

Cozy COMFORT

Transform your old sweaters into decorative pillows for your home.

Rather than discarding your favorite old sweater that's damaged from moths or too much wear, convert it into a cozy pillow. Add interest by positioning a button edge down the middle of the pillow, or place a ribbed edge as a closure to one side.

Choose a pillow form to fit the salvageable areas of the sweater, working around damage or stains. Stuff odd-shaped pillows with shredded foam. Replace plain buttons with antique ones available at secondhand stores for 25 cents to $3.

STEP-BY-STEP

1 CUT a pattern out of paper to conform to the pillow form. (Do not fit the pattern too tight to the form; the sweater cover should be slightly loose.) Pin pattern to sweater front, and zigzag stitch around pattern before cutting to prevent raveling. Carefully cut out pillow front around zigzag. Repeat process for sweater back.

2 WITH right sides together, machine-stitch the front to the back, leaving one end open to fill with pillow form. Turn right side out, and insert form; then hand-sew to close. If you choose to use the button edge of the sweater on the pillow, you can insert the pillow form at that opening.

3 HAND-SEW antique buttons to replace original ones, or add buttons to the ribbed edges for a decorative closure.

The bottom ribbed edge of two sweaters serves as side closures for pillows. Decorative buttons complete the look. Soft, cream-colored cashmere is fashioned into a simple square. The slender pillow is made from a cotton vest. The ribbed armhole edge finishes the two sides.

Lovely LINENS

These embellished pillowcases were made by sewing

on ribbon and buttons in coordinating colors.

The neckroll was created from a king-size pillowcase.

With a few yards of ribbon and some decorative buttons, you can dress your bed in luxurious linens. Simply add ribbon and buttons to pillowcases to create interesting designs. Crisp white works well, but you may want to choose a coordinating color (as we did here with soft yellow). To make a no-sew neckroll, use a king-size case and quilt batting.

Before shopping for supplies, measure the amount of ribbon needed for each pillowcase, and decide how many buttons you would like. Select grosgrain or satin ribbon, and prewash dark colors so the dye will not run onto the case when it is washed.

Tip: It takes 41 inches of ribbon to go around a standard pillowcase. We used 1 yard, 6 inches of French wire ribbon for each bow around the neckroll.

STEP-BY-STEP (PILLOWCASE)

1 DECIDE on the placement of the ribbon, and secure with straight pins. When wrapping ribbon around the pillowcase, fold edges under and meet at the side seam. Machine-stitch ribbon into place, or hand-tack with a needle and thread. Hem any loose ends, such as ties.

2 SEW on buttons.

STEP-BY-STEP (NECKROLL)

1 CHOOSE a king-size pillowcase, and press with starch. Cut 1-inch-thick batting the same size as the pillowcase, and slide batting inside.

2 STARTING with the open end, roll the pillowcase firmly but not too tightly.

3 TIE ribbon around each end of the roll to secure. French wire ribbon (1½ to 2 inches) works well for this. To wash pillowcase, simply remove the ribbons and batting.

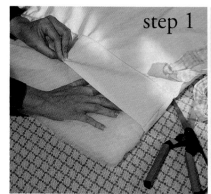 step 1
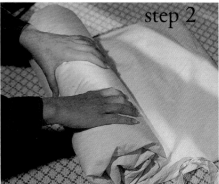 step 2
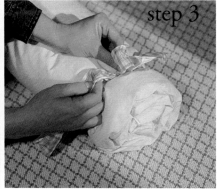 step 3

SHEER DELIGHTS

If you can tie a scarf, you can garnish a pillow with gossamer fabric.

Give a new twist to an unadorned pillow by making a cover-up improvised from sheer fabric.

All the edges of each fabric piece are simply folded under—this is definitely a no-sew project. You can create different looks by varying the length of the pieces you cut; just make them a uniform 54 inches in width, and they'll be the right dimension for wrapping an 18-inch-square pillow. Because the fabric is tied and pinned in place, it's easy to change with the seasons and alter the covering when you bring home a new fabric.

Getting Started

TOOLS & MATERIALS

18- x 18-inch velvet pillows

scissors

sheer fabrics

safety pins

ribbon or trim

IDEAS THAT WORK
•Wrap the pillows with wide velvet ribbons for additional color interest.

•When combining strips of three sheer fabrics on one pillow, try braiding them together.

•Patterned pillows can be wrapped with sheer fabrics in solid colors.

This velvet pillow gains dimension from a single strip of sheer, patterned fabric pleated and tied into a large rosette. To make a pillow like this one, use the instructions for pillow number 3; simply make tiny pleats at the center before tying the fabric ends together.

Sheer gold and floral fabrics tie together on this velvet pillow. Create the effect by following instructions for pillow number 3 but use two fabrics instead of one.

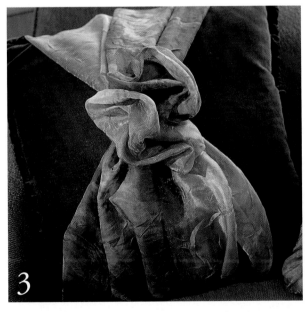

A soft pouf of fabric trims this velvet cushion. Cut two 24-inch-long pieces of 54-inch-wide fabric. Place each one facedown, side by side, on the table. Fold about 3 inches of fabric on each cut edge toward the center. Place the pillow in the center of the fabric strips and pull the folds up to form a cluster or rosette at the middle of the pillow. Tie off with a strip of trim or ribbon underneath the rosette.

To create this look, place a velvet pillow in the center of a 54- x 54-inch piece of fabric. Wrap the pillow like a gift package; then bring the ends of the fabric around to the front and knot them in the center. Turn the excess fabric to the underside of the wrapping and pin it in place. Roll a contrasting strip of 24- x 54-inch fabric and tie it across the first knot you made. Use safety pins to keep raw edges in place.

Give It a REST

Your bedroom is the place to use colors and fabrics that reflect your personal taste, for a decor that's at once soothing yet invigorating. On the following pages, we share some ideas for accessories to fill your haven with comforting style.

DESIGNER FABRICS
On Display

Don't be afraid to mix fabrics and create your own style.

It's a fabric lover's dream—a beautiful master bedroom decorated with an assortment of luxurious material. Linda Abernathy, designer of the bedroom, pulled together a grouping of stately fabrics for the room's furnishings. Soft, plush chenilles and richly textured tapestries prevail in colors of gold, wine, black, and teal.

The bedroom's centerpiece is the tapestry-covered headboard trimmed in gold chenille cording, which was made from a kit. Gold silk-flanged pillow shams shimmer against the headboard and provide a backdrop for richly colored pillows in a wide variety of shapes and hues.

Linda designed the fitted bedspread to match the trim and fabric of the headboard and set a motif for the coordinating window treatments. A gathered bed skirt made from gold silk adds the finishing touch. The same gold silk is used in full-length panels for the bedroom's four windows. The panels hang from black iron rods and rings and are paired with Roman shades in the coordinating tapestry fabric.

A gold silk bed skirt adds shimmer against the rich tones of a custom-made bedspread.

Contrasting with the deep colors of the bed and windows are the muted golds, greens, and reds of a comfy ottoman and an oversize chair. Covered in a plush chenille and trimmed in burgundy cording, the generously sized pair beckons for an afternoon of reading and hot tea. As a bonus, the ottoman is set on wheels for easy movement, and its lid lifts for ample storage.

Linda chose a wealth of accessories to complement the master bedroom. Bamboo tables and cherry-finished chests of drawers lend warmth to the room.

(TOP) An array of elegant trims dresses up this grouping of pillows.

(LEFT) The soft chenille on this ottoman and oversize chair makes for a comfortable reading spot.

Hem sheer fabric and place
it atop your comforter for an
instant style change.

Quick & Easy
BED TOPPER

Adding sheer fabric over your existing comforter will give your bed a fresh new look.

A bedding makeover can be easy with the addition of a topper. Sew a pretty piece to lie on top of your existing comforter using fabric that is sheer like the one pictured here or made out of a contrasting fabric for dramatic appeal. We chose a toile pattern, which adds a pastoral pattern to a neutral comforter.

Another way to dramatically update your bedding is to fashion new accent pillows. Basic pillow patterns can be personalized to fit the look of your bedding. An instant makeover can be achieved with minimal sewing.

Pillows created from a pattern were customized with fringe and coordinating fabric.

STEP-BY-STEP (BED TOPPER)

1 SELECT a fabric after measuring your comforter's length and width. We used approximately 6 yards for the queen-size bed shown. You will use the full 54-inch width of approximately 3 yards of fabric for the center. Cut the remaining fabric in half lengthwise for the side panels.

2 ATTACH panels at the selvages with a straight stitch, and press to one side.

3 SEW a 1½-inch double hem, and then add topstitching to ensure a flat hem.

STEP-BY-STEP (PILLOWS)

1 ASSEMBLE a pillow from the pattern of your choice.

2 CUSTOMIZE your pillow once you have sewn the body of the pillow. We suggest applying fringe or coordinating panels.

To apply double fringe, use Stitch Witchery between the two fringes. To secure, place a warm iron on the top fringe for several seconds. Then sew the double fringe to the pillow as desired.

To apply a coordinating fabric panel, cut panel in the desired shape and size, and apply Stitch Witchery to edges to hold them in place. Finish by securing the edges with a straight stitch.

Artfully draped quilts add color, pattern, and a touch of informality to this daybed.

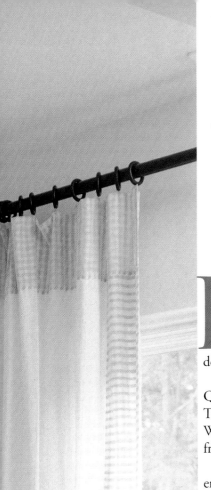

BEDCLOTHES

Lavish use of simple fabrics endows each of these beds

with a pleasing sense of enclosure.

How nice it would be to curl up for a long nap in one of these inviting beds. Designer Linda Woodrum of Hilton Head Island, South Carolina, used an abundance of white fabric to give each one a well-dressed, luxurious look. You can readily find similar materials in a neighborhood fabric shop, department store, or hardware store.

QUEEN FOR A DAY

The daybed was made by attaching twin headboards to the ends of a metal bedframe. White gauze forms the corona (or crown), a classic treatment in which fabric suspended from a central point on the ceiling drapes over the head and foot of the bed.

This effect is achieved by covering a 12-inch circle of plywood with a piece of gathered fabric; raw edges are stapled to one side. Lengths of gauze are sewn together to give the desired fullness, then hemmed at sides and bottom. Next, the top edge of the gauze is stapled to the fabric-covered plywood. The plywood is then centered over the daybed, raised to the ceiling, and nailed in place. The fabric is arranged in soft folds at the head and foot of the daybed.

All raw edges were stapled to the side of the plywood circle that meets the ceiling. Dainty edging trims the gauze.

FIT FOR A KING

(RIGHT) Standard white metal curtain rods are cut and joined to form a light-weight, 12-inch-deep framework that's the same width as the bed. It hangs from wires attached to substantial screw eyes inserted into the ceiling. White sheeting trimmed in black chintz is gathered onto the rods. A 24-inch-wide piece of white fabric, cut to have a curved lower edge and also trimmed in black, is used for the front hanging; matching ties and trim are made from black chintz.

SWEET DREAMS

(BELOW) Inexpensive mosquito netting from a bedding shop creates a misty, romantic bed surround. The airy and open look of the gauzy fabric is particularly well suited to a smaller room. The windows are equally atmospheric when hung with loosely woven curtain panels that allow natural light to pour in. Mount blinds behind the fabric to provide privacy when needed.

Black accents in art, pillows, and fabrics strengthen this bedroom's soft blue-and-white palette.

DRESS a Duvet in STYLE

Wrap your comforter with a cover that's dazzling in detail.

Using a duvet cover protects your investment in a comforter because you can remove the cover for laundering. It also makes it easy for you to change the look of a bedroom to suit the temperature outdoors. Sew a cover for summer in toile de Jouy. Then sew a cover for winter in a bold check.

STEP-BY-STEP

1 MEASURE duvet. Standard duvet sizes are as follows: twin, 68 inches x 86 inches; full or queen, 86 inches x 86 inches; king, 86 inches x 104 inches. Add 4 inches to each dimension for seam allowances and ease in duvet cover top. From full width of decorator fabric, cut 1 piece to this length for center panel. For desired width of cover top, cut 2 side panels from remaining decorator fabric, matching patterns across seams. For twin, cut 2 (10- x 90-inch) panels. For full or queen, cut 2 (19- x 90-inch) panels. For king, cut 2 (28- x 90-inch) panels.

2 STITCH 1 side panel to each side of center panel (Diagram A), with right sides together and raw edges aligned. (Note: All seams are ½ inch.) On each side edge of cover top, turn under ¾ inch twice; topstitch.

To secure duvet, cover back has 1 (7-inch-deep) flap at each side opening. To measured length of duvet, add 4 inches for seam allowances and ease. To measured width, add 18 inches for seam allowances, ease, and flaps. From full width of lining fabric, cut 1 piece to this length for center panel. For desired width of cover back, cut 2 side panels from remaining lining fabric. For twin, cut 2 (17 inch x 90 inch) panels. For full or queen, cut 2 (26- x 90-inch) panels. For king, cut 2 (35 inch x 90 inch) panels. With right sides together and raw edges aligned, stitch 1 lining side panel to each side of lining center panel for cover back. On each side of cover back, turn under ¾ inch twice; topstitch.

Diagram A

Getting Started

TOOLS & MATERIALS

54-inch-wide decorator fabric: 6 yards for twin, full, or queen; 8½ yards for king

54-inch-wide lining fabric: 5¼ yards for twin; 7¾ yards for full, queen, or king

10 (1⅛-inch) buttons (for button closure only)

Heavyweight fusible interfacing (for button closure only)

Duvet or down-filled comforter

Note: Fabric requirements include allowance for matching fabric repeats across seams and for making ties used in tie closure. Each panel in cover top is cut 90 inches long.

3 CENTER top on back, with right sides together and raw edges at head and foot aligned; pin. To form flap at each side edge, turn excess back over hemmed side edge of top, aligning raw edges at head and foot (Diagram B). Using ½-inch seams, stitch head and foot edges of cover top and back together, catching flaps in seams. Press seams flat.

4 TURN cover to right side. Tuck each flap inside. Press seamed edges flat. Topstitch seams at head and foot ¾ inch from edge, enclosing seam allowance inside stitching (Diagram C).

5 FOR BUTTON CLOSURES, MARK placement of buttonholes 14½ inches apart along each hemmed side edge of cover top. From interfacing, cut 10 (3-inch) squares. Position interfacing on wrong side of cover top to correspond with buttonhole placement marks. Following manufacturer's instructions, fuse interfacing in place. Make 1⅛-inch buttonholes in cover top at marks, perpendicular to hemmed edges. Mark corresponding button placement on flaps. Stitch buttons in place (Diagram D).

6 FOR TIE CLOSURES, MARK placement of ties 14½ inches apart along each hemmed side edge of cover top and along each folded edge of flap on cover back.

To make ties, from remaining decorator fabric, cut 20 (3 inch x 18 inch) strips. For each, with wrong sides together and raw edges aligned, fold in half lengthwise; crease. Unfold. On short ends, turn under ½ inch. Then fold long raw edges to crease at center. Refold along center crease, enclosing all raw edges. Topstitch along edges. Stitch 1 tie to cover top and back at each mark (Diagram E). Insert duvet in finished cover, tucking each side edge of duvet into flap. Button or tie cover in place.

Diagram B

Diagram C

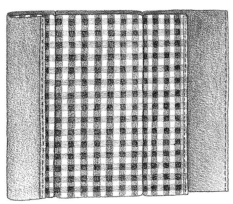

Diagram D

Diagram E

DRESS A DRESSING TABLE

Add a touch of luxury to your bedroom
by covering a table with fabric.

You'll sometimes come across old-fashioned, kidney-shaped dressing tables in secondhand-furniture stores. This new one was purchased for approximately $60 at an unfinished-furniture store. By adding a soft and graceful skirt, a glass top, and a few accessories to the table, you can create a glamorous dressing area in a corner of your bedroom.

The skirt is 3 inches longer than floor length, so it has a pleasing fullness. It's gathered on shirring tape and attached to the dressing table with self-fastening strips.

A separate fabric top fits the contours of the table. Matching cording and tucked fabric give the top its dressmaker detailing. Because the selvage is attractively fringed, it's used as trim.

Familiarize yourself with the instructions on page 136 before you begin. If you've already done some sewing for your home, you'll probably find this project to be a fairly comfortable undertaking.

Getting Started

TOOLS & MATERIALS

tape measure

fabric

thread

kraft paper

crayon

scissors

straight pins

cording

sewing machine

iron

needle

shirring tape

self-fastening strips (such as Velcro)

staple gun and staples

glass top

The fringed edge of the fabric makes a clever trim for tucks at the top of the skirt. A piece of glass protects the fabric top. Choose a comfortable stool or a small chair to place in front of your dressing table.

1 MEASURE the tabletop from left to right, and add a foot. To this measurement, add 2½ times the circumference of your table. The total equals the amount of fabric you need to buy. Choose fabric at least 54 inches wide. If it has a pattern, make sure it can be placed with the selvages running horizontally. This will enable you to make the skirt according to these directions.

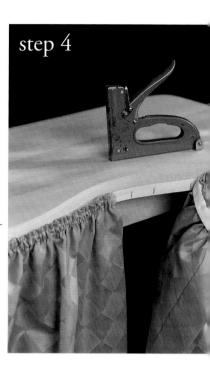

step 4

2 MEASURE from the floor to the point where you'll attach the skirt to the table. Add 4 inches for hem and 3 inches to give the skirt extra length and softness. This figure is the total length of the piece of fabric to cut for the skirt. The width of the fabric should be equal to 2½ times the circumference of the table. Cut a piece of fabric to these dimensions. (Remember, the selvage will run horizontally on the table skirt.)

3 TURN under ½ inch of fabric on each short side, and press. Again on each short side, turn 2 inches of fabric to the underside, and press. Stitch folds by hand. (These folds will eventually be positioned at center front of table.) At bottom edge of skirt, turn under ½ inch of fabric, and press. Again at bottom edge, turn 4 inches of fabric to the underside, press, and pin in place. Stitch hem by hand in the same way that you would hem a dress.

4 SEW shirring tape to top of skirt. Draw up threads in shirring tape, and adjust skirt to fit table. Check skirt for fit; then knot threads. Roll up shirring threads, and sew them in place. Measure top edge of table skirt. Cut a self-fastening strip to this measurement; separate it into two strips. Sew "hook" strip to wrong side of gathered edge of table skirt. Beginning at center front, staple "loop" strip to edge of dressing table. Again at center front, attach skirt to table by pressing "hook" strip to "loop" strip.

5 PLACE kraft paper on the tabletop. With a crayon, draw the outline of the table. Make a pattern by cutting along this line. Pin the pattern lengthwise on the fabric, and cut the fabric 1 inch outside the pattern edge. (Save the pattern for Step 9.)

step 8

6 MEASURE outside edge of pattern, add 2 inches, and cut a piece of cording to this measurement. From the scraps of fabric left from cutting the top, cut enough 1½-inch-wide bias (diagonal) strips to cover the cording. Place a pair of bias strips right sides together, and stitch along the short edges. Continue sewing bias strips together, making a piece long enough to cover the cording. Place the cording in the center of the bias strip. Fold the strip over the cording so that the right side of the fabric is on the outside. Machine-stitch alongside the cording.

7 PIN covered cording to edge of skirt top, placing line of stitching on cording 1 inch from edge of fabric. Cording should turn toward center of skirt top. Ends of cording should cross and turn toward edge of skirt top. Machine-stitch over stitching line in cording.

8 CUT a strip of fabric 6 inches wide and 2½ times the circumference of the tabletop. (Use the long piece of fabric remaining after cutting skirt.) One edge of strip should be the fringed selvage. (Or trim selvage, and press ¼ inch under; then press ½ inch under, and stitch by hand.) Starting at one short end of fabric, on side opposite the selvage, turn 1 inch of fabric to inside. Make a series of 1-inch-deep tucks that overlap each other slightly. Secure tucks with straight pins. Make a strip of tucked fabric that's long enough to extend around top. At end, turn 1 inch of fabric to underside. Check strip for fit; then stitch 1 inch from tucked edge. Beginning at center front, pin tucked edge of fabric to edge of skirt top, right sides facing. Sew along the previous line of stitching on skirt top. Remove pins. Place skirt top over tabletop.

9 TAKE the paper pattern you made for the skirt top to a glass company; have a piece of ¼-inch glass cut to this shape, and have the glass edges polished. Place glass on table.

CLEVER COVER-UP

Fabric transforms a desk and bench into a feminine dressing table set.

DISGUISING DETAILS

•For tables and desks, measure width, length, and depth for side and top panels. Sew panels together for a tailored look. Piping, trim, fringe, and decorative corner panels can be easily added to suit your style.

•Prewash fabric before sewing so it won't shrink and change shape after it's been sewn. Even slight shrinkage can completely throw off the fit.

•Protect the fabric with a glass top, available in standard sizes at home-center stores. For odd-shaped surfaces, a glass vendor can custom cut a piece.

•Slipcover patterns for standard furnishings are available from pattern manufacturers. Ask to see the craft or project patterns at your local fabric store.

Some furniture is valuable only for sentimental reasons. But there's a way to update such a piece with fabric.

Emily Reiney of Huntsville, Alabama, found a good solution for her daughter's bedroom. Emily owned perfectly functional furniture that was given to her by her father when she was a little girl—in the late sixties. Although the pieces are well loved and useful, they aren't quite the style she wants for today's look. With the creativity of local interior designer LaMerle Mikell, a few yards of fabric hide her woes.

"She couldn't just get rid of those pieces. Her father would be very disappointed," says LaMerle. "We had already selected bedding fabric that we loved," she explains, "so we just decided to dress some of the furnishings too." And because fabric can be changed easily and inexpensively, one day Emily's grandchildren may enjoy her father's purchase of long ago.

OLD LAMPS SHINE LIKE *NEW*

Follow these simple steps to spruce up old lampshades with two different looks.

Vintage lamps, easily found at flea markets, antique stores, and even in grandmothers' attics, can become new again. Attach fabric to old or inexpensive paper shades for a quick and easy project. Or use basic hand-sewing skills to gather a skirt of fabric to camouflage a plain shade. Follow the steps below to transform a lampshade of your own.

STEP-BY-STEP (CHENILLE SHADE)

1 LAY fabric right side down on a cutting surface. Place the shade, turned on its side, on the fabric, and mark with a paper clip where the shade touches the fabric. Roll the shade over the fabric until the paper clip has reached the fabric again. (This measures the circumference, which determines the width of the fabric.) Cut fabric with a ½-inch allowance. Measure the shade's length, and add 1½ inches to determine the length of the fabric. (Note: This measurement process will work only with a drum-shaped shade.)

2 PLACE fabric right side down on a large piece of paper in a well-ventilated area. Lightly mist the back side of the fabric with spray adhesive. Put the shade on the fabric, allowing a ¾-inch overhang at the top and bottom. Roll the shade over the fabric to adhere it.

3 FOLD under the allowance where the ends of the fabric meet vertically, allowing the folded edge to overlap the raw edge slightly. Hot-glue the folded edge in place to create the seam.

4 FOLD top and bottom edges of the fabric to the inside of the shade, and attach with hot glue.

(ABOVE) Chenille fabric adorns this old lampshade. The drum shape, now stylish again, sets off the wavy pattern of the fabric.

(BELOW) A wooden candle holder, wired for electricity, is the base for this lamp. The gathered fabric cover dresses a plain paper shade.

STEP-BY-STEP (GATHERED SKIRT SHADE)

1 MEASURE the circumference of the bottom of the shade. Multiply that number by 1½ to determine the fabric's width. Measure shade from top to bottom, and add 2½ inches (for hemming) to determine the length of the fabric.

2 TURN edges under ¼ inch and then ½ inch, and hand-stitch the hem on four sides. To gather the top edge, make a running stitch ½ inch from top. Begin by winding plenty of thread around a pin at the starting point to hold it. Make a line of stitches in small, neat, equal lengths. Finish by winding the thread around a second pin. Pull the threads, pushing the fabric toward the center from either end until the gathered length equals the circumference of the top of the shade, plus 1 inch. Knot the ends of the running stitch to hold the gathers in place. Sew the ends together with several stitches where the running stitch meets.

3 POSITION the skirt on the shade. Tie ribbon around the top; finish with a bow.

Stitch a Soft Throw

Fancy trims adorn a length of fabric for an elegant
throw that's "sew" easy to make.

Sewing a comfortable throw using decorative fabric is simple. Choose a reversible fabric, such as the blue-and-cream floral shown here. Lightweight woolen dress fabric and heavy, coarsely woven cotton upholstery fabric are ideal. Crumple the fabric to make sure it doesn't wrinkle easily. Select a tassel fringe with a decorative heading (the flat tape at the top) that measures at least 1 inch wide.

Getting Started

TOOLS & MATERIALS
1½ yards of 54-inch-wide reversible fabric
12⅓ yards of tassel fringe
thread
needles
straight pins

STEP-BY-STEP

1 TRIM the selvages from the fabric.

2 PIN the heading of the fringe to the fabric's edge, positioning the heading to cover the raw edge of the fabric. At the corners, fold the heading at a 45-degree angle to make it lie flat. Turn the cut ends of the fringe to the underside. By hand, baste the fringe to the fabric. Remove the pins.

3 TURN the fabric over and repeat step 2, positioning the fringe so that the top and bottom edges of the heading are perfectly aligned with the edges of the heading on the other side. Machine-stitch along the top and bottom edges of the headings so that the raw edges of the fabric are encased in the headings. Remove the basting threads.

(LEFT) Choose a reversible fabric, such as this cotton floral, that will complement the colors in your room. This fabric is a matelassé, a double cloth that's woven to look quilted. The resulting pattern is usually floral or geometric.

(RIGHT) Place the fringe so that the tassels on one side of the throw fill the spaces left by the tassels on the other side. Fold the heading down at the corners to create a 45-degree angle.

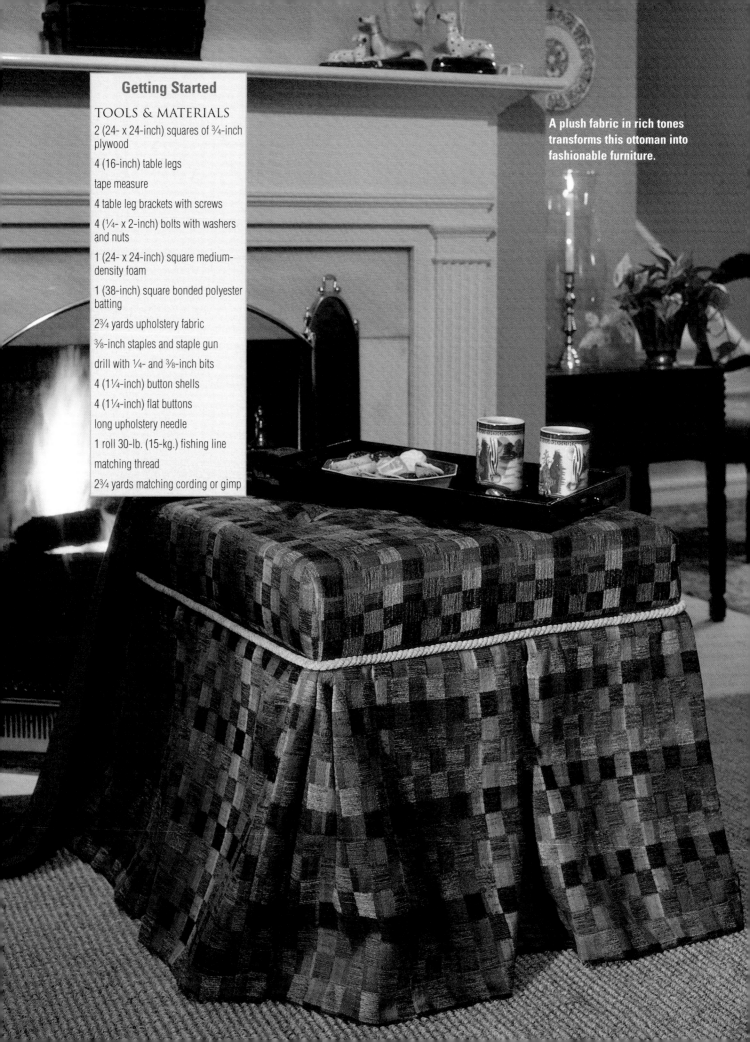

A plush fabric in rich tones transforms this ottoman into fashionable furniture.

REST *for* SOLES

step 1

Construct an ottoman with decorator fabric and a few basic materials. Then sit back and enjoy your handiwork.

step 8

Ottomans aren't just for tired feet. This large piece can double as a small coffee table, is comfortable enough to serve as extra seating, and can act as a focal point in a cheerless corner. The secret of the easy construction is two plywood squares and four prefabricated legs.

STEP-BY-STEP

1 ASSEMBLE the base by attaching the 4 legs. Using 1 plywood square, measure 6½ inches from each corner, and secure the leg brackets with the screws provided. Screw on the legs tightly.

2 DRILL a ¼-inch hole, 5 inches from the edge, in the middle of each side on the second square of plywood. These 4 holes are for fastening the decorative buttons on top of the ottoman.

3 PLACE 1 plywood square on top of the other, lining up the edges. Drill a ⅜-inch hole 8 inches from each corner, through both squares. Be careful not to drill into the ottoman's legs. Place a washer on each bolt, and insert the bolts into the holes in the top square only; screw on the nuts to temporarily hold bolts in place.

step 8

4 POSITION the foam over the top square, covering bolt heads. Place the batting over foam, and cover with a 38-inch square cut from the fabric. Pull fabric tight and staple to bottom of the top square.

5 COVER the 4 button shells with fabric. Thread the long needle with a yard or more of fishing line. Leaving a long end of line under the plywood, push needle up through one of the ¼-inch holes in the plywood. Work through foam, batting, and fabric until needle comes out the top. Thread the needle through the back of a covered button, and push back down through the same ¼-inch hole. (It may take a few tries to locate hole.) Cut the line to remove the needle. Thread the 2 long ends of the fishing line through the holes of a flat button, and pull tight. (Hint: This requires two people—one to push the button down and another to pull the fishing line.) Tie 2 or 3 square knots, and trim the ends of the fishing line. Repeat with remaining 3 buttons.

6 CUT 3 (20-inch) strips across the width of the fabric, to make the skirt. With matching thread, sew the short sides of the strips together, using a ½-inch seam, to make 1 long strip. Position skirt around the edge of the bottom plywood square, mark the depth of the hem, and stitch. Sew the short sides of the 2 ends together, forming 1 continuous piece of fabric.

7 MAKE a 4-inch pleat (8 inches of fabric) every 12 inches on the unfinished edge of the skirt, measuring from the middle of 1 pleat to the middle of the next. Make a total of 8 pleats. Adjust the skirt to fit the base, positioning a pleat at each corner and in the middle of each side. Staple the fabric skirt to the top of the bottom plywood square.

8 PLACE the cording close to the edge of the bottom plywood square on top of the fabric. Staple, overlapping the free ends. Unscrew the nuts from the bolts in the top square, and bolt the 2 plywood squares together.

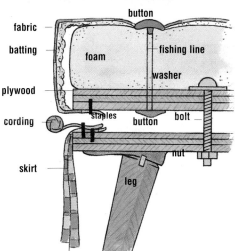

(diagram labels:) fabric, batting, foam, button, fishing line, washer, plywood, cording, staples, button, bolt, skirt, nut, leg

Fun with FABRICS

Now that your rooms are outfitted with beautifully tailored fabrics, it's time to accessorize. Choose an easy accent from the following pages for a fitting finish.

DECORATIVE PLATES

Display some of your favorite fabrics in this innovative way.

Browsing through a fabric store may be the only inspiration you need to create a charming collection of plates. By gluing fabric to the back of glass dinner plates, you can create whimsical or classic designs in a simple, affordable way. You'll find glass plates priced at $2 to $3 each. They are available at hardware and variety stores.

A little planning produces better results. First, choose a color scheme for your plates; then sketch a plan for each one.

You can easily create the look of antique china by selecting chintzes and florals that resemble actual china patterns. Combine two or more fabrics on one plate, and alternate large-scale designs with smaller prints. You'll discover many ways of making your plates interesting, both individually and as a collection.

Whether nestled in a bookcase, hung on the wall, or displayed on a table, these plates will add a perfect personal touch to any room.

Getting Started

TOOLS & MATERIALS

glass plates

paper

pencil or waterproof pen

assorted fabrics

scissors

craft knife

white craft or fabric glue

small paintbrush

liquid ravel preventer (from a fabric store)

STEP-BY-STEP

1 MAKE a paper pattern equal in size to the base of the glass plate. Trace the circular pattern onto the fabric.

2 CUT circle of fabric; brush glue onto the right side. Center it on the underside of the plate. Press out wrinkles with your fingers; let dry.

3 BRUSH a heavy layer of fabric glue onto the underside of the plate. Lay a piece of background fabric on the plate, and smooth it out. When it dries, use a craft knife to trim excess fabric along the edge of the plate. With a small brush, apply liquid ravel preventer to raw edge of fabric. Tip: Make stripes by alternating strips of contrasting fabrics. Or create a basket-weave effect by weaving strips together.

(RIGHT) Fabric-backed plates let you feature small amounts of distinctive designs. You can also repeat patterns used elsewhere in the room.

step 1

step 2

step 3

TREASURED TRANSFERS

Look around your house for artful images that, transferred onto fabric, become priceless keepsakes.

Family photographs, artwork, poetry, antique cards—your own collected treasures contain endless ideas for making fabric art. A drawing or photograph transferred to fabric takes on a gentle focus and plays with light like fine art. You can stretch the transfers on a wooden frame for a simple effect, or sew them into accent pillows. (For a framed image, you can attach picture-hanging hardware, if desired, once the frame is prepared.) Other ideas include designing pockets for shirts or sweatshirts, incorporating the transfers into place mats or afghans, or adding them to curtains or aprons.

To start, take your photos, cards, or artwork to a photocopy store. For under $20 (depending on the size) they will transfer your image in the size you request (up to 11 x 17 inches) onto the fabric you supply. Natural fabrics, such as cottons and linens, work best.

Whether you choose one project or several, your memento makeovers will add distinctive personal touches to your home, becoming not only fruits of your (quick-and-easy) labor but also the fruits of your imagination.

STEP-BY-STEP (PILLOW)

1 CHOOSE a pillow form and purchase enough linen or cotton fabric to cover the form plus ⅓ yard. Cut a piece of fabric 12 inches larger than the form for the front of the pillow. Press and roll the fabric, securing it with a rubber band for transporting. Instruct the photocopy store to color-copy your image at the size you desire onto the center of the fabric.

2 CENTER the fabric with the transfer on the pillow form; cut fabric to fit the form plus ½-inch seam allowance.

3 LAY fabric flat, taping it to a cardboard surface, and hot-glue trim around the edges of the image.

4 CUT a piece of fabric the same size as the front piece for the back of the pillow. (This includes ½-inch seam allowance.) Placing right sides together, sew front to back, leaving a 6-inch opening in the middle of one side. Insert pillow form, and stitch opening closed.

Enlarging antique seed packets and imprinting them on fabric emphasizes their aged character.

It's hard to resist a pillow adorned with the image of loved ones.

For Pillow:

pillow form

linen or cotton fabric

scissors

photograph or paper artwork

iron

rubber band

trim or ribbon

hot-glue gun and glue sticks

large piece of cardboard

sewing machine

thread to match fabric

For Framed Image:

photograph or paper artwork

scissors

cotton duck fabric

iron

rubber band

4 stretcher strips

staple gun and staples

acrylic gel medium

1-inch paintbrush

picture-hanging hardware (optional)

Copying photos onto cotton duck
softens the play of light, creating
a sumptuous scene.

150

STEP-BY-STEP (FRAMED IMAGE)

step 2

1 CHOOSE a photo or paper artwork and determine what size you want the finished image to be. Cut a piece of cotton duck 18 inches wider and 18 inches deeper than the desired image size. Press and roll the fabric (to prevent wrinkling), securing with a rubber band for transporting. Instruct the photocopy store to color-copy the image at the size you desire onto the center of the fabric.

2 ASSEMBLE a frame, using stretcher strips, that is approximately 8 inches larger than the image size. Lay fabric, image side down, on a clean, flat surface. Center the frame over the image area. Stretch fabric over strips, and staple into place, beginning with one staple in the center of each side. Continue stretching and stapling the remaining fabric, tucking folds neatly at the corners.

3 BRUSH acrylic gel medium on the front and sides of framed image. Allow gel medium to dry, and apply a second coat. This will protect the image and give the piece the look of a painting.
Note: Special permission is required to reproduce published material.

SUITABLE *for* FRAMING

It's easy to transform a handsome towel into an attractive wall hanging.

I f you need a piece of artwork for your kitchen or breakfast room, buy an intricately woven, cotton damask towel. By choosing a mat and molding that complement the towel and are appropriate for your room, you can create a unique framed image.

You'll find damask towels in kitchen shops and mail-order catalogs that sell fine linens. These towels often bear designs of vegetables, fruit, or flowers, and are available in various colors. Elaborate borders and backgrounds add to their individuality.

1 IRON the towel, using spray starch to remove any folds. Place the starched towel between pieces of poster board to prevent wrinkles, and take it to a frame shop.

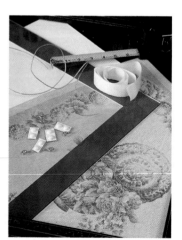

2 SELECT a combination of mat board and picture-frame molding that best displays your towel, and then have the towel framed.

Getting Started

TOOLS & MATERIALS
iron
cotton damask towel
spray starch
2 pieces of poster board

NEW & NOTEWORTHY

Turn a plain bulletin board into an extraordinary accent piece.

Looking for ways to organize your life? A bulletin board for important letters and notes will help clear your desktop or kitchen counter. Tuck in a few favorite snapshots for a personal touch.

With the addition of fabric and ribbon, an ordinary bulletin board becomes a choice interior accent. First, select a framed bulletin board in a size to fit your space. Purchase enough batting and fabric to cover the front of the board (allow a few inches of fabric to fold to the back). Using a measuring tape, determine the yardage needed for the diagonal strips of ribbon. Choose a ribbon color to complement your fabric choice. Follow the step-by-step instructions to complete your note board.

STEP-BY-STEP

1 CUT a single layer of batting to fit over the cork board inside the frame.

2 POSITION the fabric over the bulletin board, leaving about a 2-inch overhang of fabric on all four sides. Turn the board over, and pull fabric tightly. Then fold the edges under and staple to wooden frame. (Secure opposite ends first.)

3 LAY grosgrain ribbon from one corner to opposite corner of board. Continue laying diagonal strips of ribbon spaced equally apart. Create a diamond pattern by laying ribbon diagonally in opposite directions. Secure with decorative upholstery tacks at intersections of ribbon. Turn board over and staple ribbons to back of wooden frame; cut off excess.

step 1

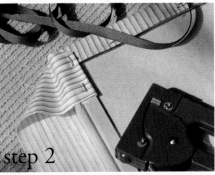

step 2

step 3

CANVAS ORGANIZER

Tie a clever canvas organizer to a door with string, or hang grommets from cup hooks. Now your supplies are easily accessible.

Coordinate craft supplies, garden tools, or toys with this easy-to-make organizer. Made from a heavy cotton known as canvas or cotton duck, this fabric is durable and affordable. Basic sewing skills are all you need to create this project in an afternoon.

Getting Started

TOOLS & MATERIALS

1 yard of solid canvas fabric

1 yard of striped canvas fabric

measuring tape

scissors

4 (1-inch) grommets

thread to match fabric

self-fastening strips (such as Velcro)

sewing machine

STEP-BY-STEP

1 CUT the fabric for the background panel 28 inches x 48 inches. (This includes a 3-inch hem allowance on each side.) Turn edges under 3 inches, and press. Turn edges again 1½ inches, and press. Open all the folds. To miter the corners, fold each one diagonally where the first fold intersects, and press. Open out and trim along the diagonal fold. Fold diagonally again where the second fold intersects, press, and fold each side over twice along original fold lines, and pin in place. Stitch hem 1¼ inches from edge. (See illustrations at right.)

2 CUT the large pocket from a striped canvas 24 inches x 23 inches. Fold in half (creating a 24- x 11½-inch panel), right sides together. Stitch the long side with a ½-inch seam. (Leave short ends open.) Turn right side out, and press. Turn raw edges under ½ inch, and press. Pin to the canvas back, lining up bottom and side edges, making the fold the top of the pocket. Topstitch the pocket to the back ¼ inch from edge. Topstitch vertically up the center of the panel to create two pockets.

3 CUT another piece of striped fabric 17 inches x 9 inches. Fold in half (creating a 17- x 4½-inch panel), right sides together. Stitch the long side with a ½-inch seam. (Leave short ends open.) Turn right side out, and press. Turn raw edges under ½ inch, and press. Pin pocket panel to the canvas back 14 inches from the bottom, and line up with the right side, making the fold the top of the pocket. Topstitch the pocket to the back ¼ inch from edge. Topstitch twice vertically up the panel, 5⁶⁄₁₆ inches apart, to create three pockets.

4 CUT a piece of natural-colored canvas 5½ inches x 9 inches. Fold in half (creating a 5½- x 4½-inch panel), right sides together. Stitch the long side with a ½-inch seam. (Leave short ends open.) Turn right side out, and press. Turn raw edges under ½ inch, and press. Pin pocket panel to the canvas back 14 inches from the bottom, and line up with the left side and the pocket panel just attached, making the fold the top of the pocket. Topstitch the pocket to the back ¼ inch from edge. Topstitch three times vertically up the panel, 1 inch apart, to create four narrow pockets.

5 CUT a piece of striped canvas 24 inches x 15 inches. Fold in half (creating a 24- x 7½-inch panel), right sides together. Stitch the long side with a ½-inch seam. (Leave short ends open.) Turn right side out, and press. Turn raw edges under ½ inch, and press. Pin panel to the canvas back 21 inches from the bottom, and line up with side, making the fold the top of the pocket. Topstitch the panel to the back ¼ inch from edge. Topstitch up the panel two times, 7⁵⁄₁₆ inches apart, to create three pockets.

6 CUT a piece of striped canvas 13 inches x 5 inches. (This time we turned the stripes vertically.) Fold in half (creating a 13- x 2½-inch panel), right sides together. Stitch the long side with a ½-inch seam. (Leave short ends open.) Turn right side out, and press. Turn raw edges under ½ inch, and press. Pin panel to the canvas back, 34 inches from the bottom and lined up with the left side, making the fold the top of the pocket. Topstitch the panel to the back, on short ends only ¼ inch from edge. Topstitch vertically up the panel four times, 2¼ inches apart, to create five open loops.

MITERING CORNERS
STEP 1

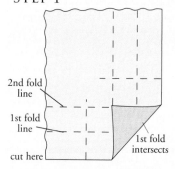

2nd fold line

1st fold line

cut here

1st fold intersects

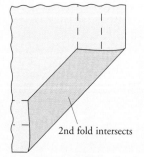

2nd fold intersects

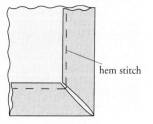

hem stitch

7 CUT a piece of striped fabric 12 inches x 5 inches. Fold in half (creating a 12- x 2½-inch panel), right sides together. Stitch the long side with a ½-inch seam. (Leave short ends open.) Turn right side out, and press with the seam in the middle of panel. Tuck raw edges of short sides to the inside ½ inch, and pin. Topstitch all four sides of strip ¼ inch from edge. Sew a 1- x 1⅛-inch self-fastening strip to one end of strip on the seam side. Securely attach the other end, seam side up, to the back, 6 inches from top and 4 inches from right edge, with a zigzag stitch. Sew mate side of self-fastening strip to the back panel 2 inches above zigzag stitch.

8 PUNCH four 1-inch grommets through the fabric, following the manufacturer's instructions. Position the grommets across the panel ¼ inch from top. Finished size is 22 x 42 inches.

TEXTILE TERMS

Fabrics come in a host of colors, finishes, textures, and raw materials. These terms relate to the types and uses of various textiles.

BATTENBERG LACE: A type of Renaissance lace made from linen braid or linen thread and crafted together to create detailed patterns. Can be machine made or handmade.

BIRD'S-EYE: Either linen or cotton cloth characterized by a small geometric pattern with a center dot.

BROADCLOTH: A tightly woven cotton fabric with delicate embedded crosswise ribs that resembles poplin. Originally a fabric made on a loom wider than 27 inches.

BROCADE: A richly heavy, interwoven fabric with a raised floral pattern or figurative design. Features an embossed appearance by contrasting textures, colors, and gold or silver threads.

BUNTING: A cotton or worsted cloth with a plain, open weave, similar in texture to a scrim or cheesecloth. Often dyed bold colors and used for flags, banners, and other festive decorations.

BURLAP: Coarse canvas fabric made from jute, hemp, or cotton.

CALICO: An inexpensive, tightly woven cotton. Usually brightly printed cloth on a white or contrasting background. One of the oldest basic cotton fabrics.

CHALLIS: A soft, lightweight fabric with a plain weave printed with delicate patterns of flowers. Originally made of wool, but now available in cottons, rayon, and blends.

CHINO: A traditional, 100% twilled, cotton fabric made of combed two-ply yarns and vat-dyed khaki.

CHINTZ: Highly glazed cotton fabric generally woven with a hard spun fine warp. Usually printed with bold floral patterns, stripes, or figurative designs in bright colors.

CRINOLINE: A firm or highly sized fabric used to bolster the edge of a hem or puffed sleeve.

CUT VELVET: Velvet fabric with a cutout design or pile effect. Patterns and colors can be elaborate.

DAMASK: A stiff, glossy fabric with a textured pattern. Similar to brocade, but the pattern is usually reversible and less pronounced. Although originally from China, the fabric was first introduced to Europe through Damascus, hence its name.

DOWN: Lightweight and soft, fluffy underfeathers of water fowl, duck, and geese. Used for stuffing pillows and comforters.

FELT: A matted and compact woolen material either woven or unwoven.

GABARDINE: Sturdy, tightly woven fabric that features a decided diagonal line, either on a 45-degree or 63-degree twill, on the face of the cloth. Can be made from most major fibers or blends; fabric wears well because of twist in the yarns and the texture.

HERRINGBONE TWILL: Fabric with a broken twill weave composed of vertical sections that are alternately right hand and left hand in direction that produces a zigzag effect.

HOUNDSTOOTH: A wool cloth distinguished with a medium-size, broken check pattern. The color is surrounded by white yard, and the check resembles a four-pointed star.

MATELASSÉ: A soft, cushioned or padded fabric. A double-cloth cotton fabric with a woven textured pattern that resembles quilting. Often used for coverlets, bed linens, draperies, and upholstery.

MUSLIN: Generic term for a wide range of cotton fabrics.

ORGANDY: A fine, sheer, and wiry cotton fabric that retains crispness after laundering. Used for clothing and draperies, organdy is a true durable finish material.

ORGANZA: A light, thin, almost transparent fabric made of woven silk, rayon, or nylon and given a stiff wiry finish; similar to organdy.

PINWALE: A very narrow rib or tight ridge woven into a fabric. One common example is corduroy.

PIQUÉ: A medium or heavyweight cloth with raised cords that run in the warp direction.

REPEAT: In a printed fabric, the length and width for the entire pattern before it begins again.

STRIÉ: A fabric with irregular stripes or streaks of nearly the same color.

TAFFETA: A thin, plain woven fabric smooth on both sides, often with a sheen on the front surface. Originally made of silk.

TICKING: Tightly woven cotton fabric commonly used for pillow and mattress covers. It often features stripes of blue, brown, gray, or red against a white background.

TOILE: Fine cretonne and linen fabrics with elaborate scenic designs and landscapes printed in a single color.

TWEED: An irregular, soft and flexible woolen fabric made of two-and-two twill weaves.

WAFFLE CLOTH: A fabric with a distinctive honeycomb pattern. Called waffle piqué when made of cotton.

WARP: The arrangement of the yarns that run vertical or longwise in woven fabrics.

A WORD ON WINDOWS

CORDING: The mechanism used to raise and lower shades; it consists of a system of cords threaded through small rings sewn onto the back of the shade.

FINISHED DROP: Shade length once it is completed and hung.

FINISHED WIDTH: The area covered by the completed shade.

INSIDE MOUNT SHADE: A shade mounted inside a window frame.

LAMBREQUIN: Similar to a cornice, a shaped form surrounding not only the top of the window frame but also the sides. Usually made from a sturdy material such as plywood or fiberboard.

LATH: A support on a shade, generally a piece of wood cut to the finished top width of the shade, functioning as a mounting device.

OUTSIDE MOUNT SHADE: A shade whose finished width is that of the window frame, mounted outside the window recess.

SUPPORT: A device used to hold a shade or curtain in position; it may be attached outside, inside, or within the frame. Examples are poles, tracks, and laths.

page 42

INDEX

page 148

page 93

page 16

ACKNOWLEDGMENTS

Linda Abernathy
Wendy Wooden Barze
Oma Blaise
Mr. and Mrs. Philip Brooks
Laurel and Louie Buntin
Melanie Clarke
Cheryl Dalton
Bitsy Duggins
Alice Elmore
Mary Leigh Fitts
Bob Gager
J. Savage Gibson
Melanie Grant
Joseph K. Hall
Isie V. Hanson
Buffy and Zeb Hargett
Brooke Hatten
Alyce Head
Dana Holcombe
Sherrill Holt
Barbara Johnson Irvine
Mary Lyn H. Jenkins
Marjorie H. Johnston
Louis Joyner
Ginger Kelly
Lynne Long
Sandra Allen Lynn
Sylvia Martin
Melanie McNiel
LaMerle Mikell
Emily Minton
Janie Molster
Duffy Morrison
Lynn Nesmith
Rose Nguyen
Ruby Norris
Pate-Meadows Designs
Emily Reiney
Lou Alice Rogers
Jennie Shannon
Tracy Sisson
Eleanor and Jim Thomason
Jose and Nerra Torres
Deborah Valentine
Jarinda S. Wiechman
Linda Woodrum

Some of the features in this work were previously published in *Decorating Step-By-Step, Southern Living*®, *Accent on Style from Hancock Fabrics*, or *Lowe's Creative Ideas for Home and Garden*.

  For more information on Hancock Fabrics products used, visit the website at *www.hancockfabrics.com*

  For more information on Lowe's products used, call 1-800-44LOWES or visit the Lowe's website at *www.Lowes.com*

Decorating Step-By-Step, published by *Southern Living*, offers ideas and projects for creative home design. You'll find complete instructions for making and using a wealth of decorative items for every room. In each issue, you'll also visit homes decorated with imagination and personal flair. Information on art, architecture, and antiques is featured, as well. And ideas for the creative preparation and serving of food flavor each issue. *Decorating Step-By-Step* is a newsstand publication, now available each May, August, and November.

page 50